The Sports Industry and Collective Bargaining

Paul D. Staudohar

ILR Press

New York State School of
Industrial and Labor Relations
Cornell University

Cover design by Kathleen Dalton

Cover photo courtesy of National Baseball Library,
Cooperstown, New York

Library of Congress number: 86-7160

ISBN: cloth, 0-87546-117-4
     paper, 0-87546-118-2

Library of Congress Cataloging in Publication Data

Staudohar, Paul D.
    The sports industry and collective bargaining.

    Bibliography: p.
    Includes index.
    1. Professional sports—United States. 2. Collective
bargaining—Sports—United States. I. Title.
GV583.S83   1986   331.89′041796   86-7160
ISBN 0-87546-117-4
ISBN 0-87546-118-2 (pbk.)

Copies may be ordered from
ILR Press
New York State School of
Industrial and Labor Relations
Cornell University
Ithaca, New York 14851-0952

Printed in the United States of America by Braun-Brumfield.
5 4 3 2 1

In memory of my grandmother, Katerina

Contents

Preface

*F*ollowers of professional sports in the print and broadcast media are aware of the increasing influence of collective bargaining. Players in the major sports leagues are well organized for negotiation with management. Unionization has accompanied the growth of the sports industry, as players strive for greater shares of gate receipts and television revenues.

This book is written for the sports fan who wants to know more about labor relations. It uses an interdisciplinary approach to examine employment in the four major professional sports—baseball, football, basketball, and hockey—and to explain the dynamics of key issues such as free agency, salaries, drug abuse, and strikes. No single approach is appropriate for viewing these issues because each has legal, economic, and psychological implications.

Earl Warren, the late chief justice of the U.S. Supreme Court, used to say that he always read the sports pages of the newspaper first because he liked to read about man's accomplishments rather than his failures. Although games were lost as often as won, players were regarded as winners. But this is no longer always true. Today, the sports pages record generous evidence of the failure of human character. Unsavory topics like greed, deceit, and cocaine keep cropping up. In a sense, the socioculture of professional sports mirrors life itself.

To the frustration of many sports fans, collective bargaining disputes resulted in long strikes in baseball in 1981 and football in 1982. Like any newly unionized industry, sports is going through a period of acrimonious confrontation between labor and management. As collective bargaining evolves, conflict should diminish, with the parties settling down to explore ways to enhance their mutual welfare. Although signs of maturity are appearing already, the adversary relationship remains prevalent.

Although this is a relatively short book, there is a long list of people who deserve thanks for their generous contributions. Since little has been written on the topic in the literature, library resources were limited. Nanette Sand and Clara Stern, librarians at the Institute of Industrial Relations at the University of California, Berkeley, were helpful in locating much of what was available. Other primary sources of information were the league and players' association offices in the respective sports and newspaper accounts. Representatives from the leagues and players' associations provided original data and helped verify materials from other published sources. In baseball, these persons were Marvin J. Miller, John J. Gaherin, Kenneth Moffett, Peter Gold, and Sue Carr. Information on football was received from Pete Rozelle, Edward Garvey, Frank Woschitz, Jack Donlan, Bob Epstein, Jay Benoit, George R. Berman, Don Weiss, and Terry Bledsoe. In basketball, thanks are due Lawrence O'Brien, Lawrence Fleisher, and Russell Granik, and in hockey, Clarence S. Campbell, John A. Ziegler, Jr., R. Alan Eagleson, S. G. Simpson, Gary Meagher, Carole Robertson, Michael Griffin, John Halligan, and Roger Gottlieb.

I would also like to express my appreciation to Colonel Edward M. Smith, United States Air Force; Margaret Magnus, editor, *Personnel Journal*; Bart Wright, sports writer, *Tacoma News-Tribune*; Christ P. Zivalich of Central Michigan University; and the late Edwin C. Pendleton of the University of Hawaii. Special thanks are due to the all-star team at ILR Press: director Frances G. Benson, editor Holly M. Bailey, and promotions associate Andrea Fleck Clardy.

Paul D. Staudohar

1. Introduction

Some people begrudge professional athletes their high salaries, yet few players feel they are overpaid. It seems unfair that Eddie Murray, a first baseman for the Baltimore Orioles, should have a yearly salary ($2.6 million) that far exceeds that of the president of the United States ($200,000). Although the astronomical salaries of so many professional athletes are a recent phenomenon, they are not without precedent. Much of the country was shocked in 1931 when baseball star Babe Ruth was offered $80,000 to play for the Yankees, while President Herbert Hoover was paid only $75,000. When Ruth was asked if he deserved to make more than the president, he is said to have replied, "Why not? I had a better year than he did."[1]

Contests in skill, strength, and speed have occupied an important place in every culture throughout the ages. But the meaning of the term sport and the effect that sport has on society are different things.[2] The characteristics of sport can be thought of as neutral or isolated qualities, devoid of implication for society. When one runs, jumps, or throws as pure sport it is an internalized response to a human desire for physical and psychological exercise. Viewed apart from social meaning, sport involves play for the body and spirit—for health and happiness. Play provides a sense of creativity and eases tensions. When sport is organized into games for competition, these events satisfy such needs as achievement, affiliation, and self-esteem.

1

Social meanings are assigned to sport by the culture. Sports that reflect high social status, such as sailboat racing, polo, and horse racing, do not have any inherent status apart from that conferred by society. Certain sports become popular because society places a high value on them. As a sport becomes institutionalized, it takes on its own meanings and values, which reflect on the society.[3] For example, American culture awards great social significance to baseball, the national pastime. That sport—from Little League to major leagues—provides play, entertainment, rules, and competition that in turn shape our culture.

American culture has a particular fascination with winning, which explains some of the attention given to competitive sports and the boom in these sports at the professional level. Yet other sports that do not emphasize winning, such as backpacking, jogging, and fishing, are also widely practiced. Much of the cultural identification with competitive sports is by spectators, who derive vicarious satisfaction from watching highly skilled athletes engage in bold and often violent competition. Few professional athletes themselves, however, identify strongly with the play element in sport. They are motivated by winning, maximization of economic reward, fear of injury, loss of skill, and achievement of personal goals. Nearly all suffer fatigue, not euphoria, from a lengthy season. They have little sense of play for the joy of it.

Professional players have become bureaucratized. They pursue their playing careers as businesses. Many players are even legally incorporated. Most of their time is spent on nonplay endeavors. Players deal with agents, who represent them in salary negotiations and commercial endorsements, and they are active in affairs of the players' associations, which attend to much of the business with the teams. The teams and the leagues they comprise are also bureaucratized. Authority for important functions at the league level is centralized in the offices of commissioners, presidents, and other governing bodies. Although team owners employ these representatives to act on their behalf, thus retaining some control over decision making, there is a system of offices that define what role each officeholder is to play, and within each team there is a hierarchy of offices and positions with specific division of work and responsibility.

Professional players, teams, and leagues have a symbiotic relationship with the print and broadcast media, which are themselves compartmentalized into specialized units. Games receive extensive coverage in newspapers and magazines and are broadcast on radio and television. Income from consumers, who pay for the use of these services, and from advertisers, who sell their wares through the media, provides impetus to the commercialization of sports. Cities take pride in their teams, and numerous satellite industries that derive substantial revenues from sports have sprung up.

The big business that the professional sports complex represents has a profound influence on cultural values, norms, and behavior in the United States. Are the effects of it positive or negative? They are both.[4] Sport for youth is generally positive, although more observers are expressing qualms about the excessive organization and competition found in youth leagues today. Team games and exercises stimulate health, comradeship, self-control, and perhaps even intelligence. Sport teaches youngsters the importance of discipline, cooperation, and how to handle winning and losing gracefully. It also provides entertainment for millions of spectators of all ages. Fans look forward to the beginning of seasonal play and enjoy following their favorite teams in competition.

On the other hand, excessive emphasis on certain aspects of sport can produce negative results. The heavy significance attached to winning creates feelings of inferiority when one loses and detracts from the joy of sport. Evidence is mounting that violence in sport promotes aggressive behavior in society, and violence by spectators at sporting events has increased dramatically in recent years. The drug abuse issue has tainted certain professional sports, and called into question the value of players as role models. Televised sports mesmerize viewers who sit for hours in their fantasy world of jock power, to the neglect of active participation in sports that promote good health. Youngsters who aspire to professional athletic careers, which can be achieved only by a tiny proportion, may neglect their education and other important aspects of normal living. Organized sport may also foster an elitism and militaristic behavior that are unhealthy in people of any age.

Spectator sport provides an outlet for viewing the vitality of youth, speed, and strength. The levels of skill displayed fascinate people. Men identify more directly than do women with spectator sport because of their childhood experience and the macho nature of physical contact games. For men there is an additional attraction in the fantasy that because they are male they could be called on to be there on field or court, asked to contribute their playing or coaching skills. Viewing sport thus provides the raw material for dreams. Nevertheless, women too feel vicarious satisfaction of a desire to win, and more women are becoming active in competitive sports. In a way, competition is life in microcosm. If only the strong survive in Spencerian competition for determining the fittest, one must do his or her part to ensure identification with winning. No one wants to be known as a loser. Of course, teams lose half the time, but losses, especially on television, can be rationalized; they are quickly forgotten. But victories are savored and remembered.

Labor relations did not play a dominant role in professional sports until the early 1970s. Although player conflicts over work practices came early in the development of professional sports, they were characterized by infrequent and transitory confrontations with team owners. In the decades before unions and collective bargaining became ingrained in the sports industry, professional athletes were treated like privileged peons. They had adulation from the public and generally made larger incomes from playing games than they would have made in outside pursuits, but hardly any made big money. Players viewed themselves as knights on a noble mission to provide entertainment and have fun in the process. They were not engaged in the contests for power with management that coal miners and steelworkers were. Sport was more avocation and pastime than career and business.

A few players thought they suffered injustice by being locked into servile relationships with tight-fisted owners who controlled their present and future. But this injustice was endured for the good of the sport these players dedicated their lives to. In any event, players had no real alternative. They could be sold, traded, and released like any other business asset. Power was exclusively in the hands of the owners, who dictated contract terms knowing that they were the sole parties the player could deal with.

By the early 1970s, growing fan interest in the games, heightened by network television, had transformed professional sports into lucrative business enterprises. Leagues expanded to take advantage of population explosions in the cities of the West and South. Wealthy business moguls bid for sports franchises as tax havens and ego builders. Entirely new leagues sprang up to compete with established organizations and lure away players at attractive salaries. As sports became more like traditional businesses, players increasingly turned to agents to represent them in individual salary negotiations. Most important, players' associations, formerly weak or nonexistent, became a countervailing power to the owners' exclusive interests. Professional sports entered a new era, featuring collective bargaining, court actions, and strikes.

Industrial Relations Models

The sports industry is a part of the larger industry providing services to entertain the American public, and labor relations in the industry comprise key components that are applicable to the industrial relations systems in any free society. This is shown by John Dunlop's classic model explaining an industrial relations system as a response to a universal labor problem, the construction of a set of acceptable rules by which the participants in productive work are related to each other.[5] An industrial relations system is designed to resolve important questions affecting work: How is work to be organized? Who is going to perform it? What standards of discipline apply at the workplace? How will the economic rewards from work be distributed among the participants? The answers to these questions are determined by rules, established by what Dunlop calls the "actors"—management, workers, and government. Management is a hierarchy of decision makers who issue instructions. Workers are also viewed as a hierarchy, which is formalized if they are represented by unions or informal if they are not. Government comprises specialized agencies that may either substantially regulate management and workers or be relatively weak and overridden by them on important issues.

Regardless of the relative power of Dunlop's three actors, they interact in an environment determined by the larger society. The principal features of this environment are technology, market constraints, and societal power. Although the actors determine the rules, the content of the rules is influenced by environmental constraints, and the actors' strategies are based in large part on changes in the environment.[6] Technology has far-reaching effects on production hardware, skills, and techniques, which in turn determine the size of the work force, its concentration in a narrow area or diffusion, and the stability of the work group. Market or budgetary constraints affect the size of the enterprises, competitive position of organizations and industries, economic expansion, and the ratio of labor costs to total costs, and these factors may force management to seek greater control over work rules. The distribution of societal power determines the actors' prestige, position, and access to ultimate authority within the larger society. Frequently, the economic power within an industrial relations system comes into conflict with the political power in a society. Workers and management seek to channel conflict into the political or economic arena in which their control is perceived to be greater.

Introduction

The vast network of industrial relations rules governs three basic subjects: (1) compensation, (2) duties and performance of workers, and (3) rights of workers in the workplace. There is considerable variation in these rules among industries and individual enterprises. Whatever their specific content, however, the detailed and technical nature of the rules tends to create a distinct group of experts or professionals for the design and administration of rules. It is not uncommon for problems of communication or conflict to arise between the experts and the rest of the hierarchy, and it is necessary to control these tensions when they occur.

Underlying the industrial relations system is a set of beliefs held by the actors, a body of common ideas that define the role of each actor and the relationships among them. A stable system implies congruence among beliefs. If views are incompatible—managers perceive workers paternalistically or workers view managers as having no useful purpose—the actors have difficulty reconciling their roles, and relationships tend to be volatile. Conflicting ideologies present a formidable challenge to the operation of industrial relations systems, as the actors search for a compatible set of ideas that recognize the needs of each.

The Entertainment Industry

Although there are many differences between sports and the other sectors of the entertainment industry, there are important similarities. The entertainment industry is a diverse amalgam of subgroups, primarily film production and distribution, radio and television broadcasting, live performing arts, and professional sports. Some observers exclude sports from the entertainment industry, focusing instead on its more traditional components, which have a long history of unionization and collective bargaining. But with the emergence of formalized union-management relations in sports, geographic expansion of the business, and heavy exposure of sporting events on television, professional sport is clearly within the ambit of the organized entertainment industry in terms of industrial relations structure and its share of the total income of the entertainment industry. Although sport competes with some segments of the entertainment industry for consumer spending, it also has a close relationship with television in presentation of live events. The televising of sporting events has increased such that a large proportion of the revenues of professional sports franchises comes from this source.

As David Tajgman observes, the demand for television programing depends on the size of the television distribution system.[7] He notes that technological developments, such as cable and pay television and direct satellite broadcasting, are expanding broadcast time and the demand for programing. This has caused organizational and revenue distribution problems for management and unions in the entertainment industry as a whole. Sport is affected because expanded broadcast of amateur and professional events has brought a mixed blessing of greater exposure to the public but decreased attention to individual events as a result of oversaturation of the market. The extent of influence that television has on sports has also changed. Schedules, locations, and times of games are readily shifted to adapt to the needs of television. Ownership of sports franchises has moved toward vertical integration; that is, sports entrepreneurs more often have ownership interests in other parts of the entertainment industry—especially in the broadcast media—so that these elements can be combined for greater income potential.

There are some interesting similarities between the labor force of the entertainment industry and that of its sports component. Management is highly dependent on the work force—live entertainment cannot go on without it. In general, workers are well educated and know how to use their economic power to greatest advantage. Both are subject to the "star system," in which exceptionally talented people dominate the worker hierarchy. Whether actors, rock musicians, or athletic superstars, these elite persons command vastly disproportionate influence on their professions and derive substantial incomes from outside sources. Although exceptionally talented performers will always be able to derive exceptional incomes, one of the important reasons that unions have arisen in sports and other segments of the entertainment industry is the need to further the economic interests of workers farther down in the hierarchy—marginal players, equipment operators, and stagehands—whose talents are more easily replaced. Along with the older unions which have long had a strong voice in the determination of institutional rules, sports unions are increasingly getting more control over the rule-making process. In seeking greater influence over membership destiny, the sports unions are following the lead of their antecedents in the entertainment industry, unions such as the Screen Actors Guild, National Association of Broadcast Engineers and Technicians, and American Federation of Television and Radio Artists.

Sports Industry Model

A simple model illustrating the key elements of labor relations in the sports industry is shown in figure 1.1. Underlying this model is the proposition that industrial relations includes the institutions, theories, and processes for resolving contending money and power claims in the employment relationship.[8] The three principal participants in the industrial relations function are government, management, and labor, and government's role is primarily that of regulator of the other two institutions.

The federal government performs the regulatory function under its legislative, executive, and judicial branches. Labor relations in sports are formalized under a system of union representation and collective bargaining, and therefore the National Labor Relations Act of 1935 provides a basic legal framework that carries with it a half-century of experience in other areas of American commerce. Hundreds of decisions by the National Labor Relations Board and federal courts, which interpret and apply the law to collec-

Figure 1.1   Model of Labor Relations in the Sports Industry

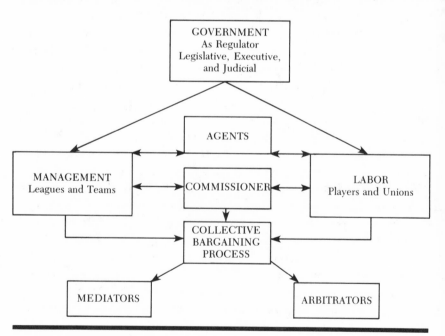

tive bargaining, right to strike, and antitrust policy, have substantial effects on the sports industry.

Management, operating through league structures and team ownership, provides for the planning, supervision, and control of corporate enterprise decisions. The leagues have responsibility for such functions as negotiating collective bargaining agreements, setting rules for drafting of players, determining policies for the enforcement of management rights, and negotiating national television agreements. Owners of clubs give up much of their authority to the league offices but retain decision-making authority in areas such as negotiating individual player contracts, movement of players to other teams (subject to the negotiated agreement with the union), hiring coaches and front office personnel, and entering into local television contracts.

Labor refers to the players and their unions. The principal objective of the sports union is to promote its effectiveness in collective bargaining. In achieving its objectives, the union (1) engages in organizing its membership for solidarity, (2) negotiates contracts applicable to all players, (3) uses pressure tactics such as strikes and picketing, if necessary, (4) enforces the terms of the negotiated agreement through the grievance procedure, and (5) serves an internal governmental function in conducting meetings, voting on contracts negotiated, and providing other means of communication to members. Since nearly all players at the major league level pay substantial dues to their unions, these organizations constitute a formidable presence in collective bargaining.

As shown in figure 1.1, there are two other participants that interact with management and labor in sports. These are the commissioner and agents. The role of the commissioner varies among sports. Theoretically, the commissioner is supposed to serve both management and labor, as well as to be a public spokesperson. As a practical matter, commissioners tend to line up more on the side of management on contentious issues. This reflects the fact that they are selected, paid, and retained at the discretion of management. Nonetheless, commissioners serve as a kind of buffer between the two sides in areas of dispute, and seek to represent the interests of both in areas of mutual benefit.

Agents, on the other hand, are clearly a thorn in the side of management. As the representatives of players in individual salary contract negotiations, agents have added a powerful impetus to raising average salaries to dizzying heights. Some agents also represent players in managing their assets and in outside commercial ventures such as television commercials. Management resents the intrusion of agents on their control over players, and some impartial observers view agents as a destructive force in sports. But their success in enhancing the economic welfare of their clients is undeniable, and agents will retain their influential role unless the players' unions take over the individual contract negotiating function. A possible compromise, which is currently being done in football and basketball, is the screening of agents to help avoid players being taken advantage of by unscrupulous agents.

The figure does not depict a role for agents in the collective bargaining process. They are involved only in the limited sense of handling individual salary negotiations, which may include incentives and bonuses but not for all players as a group. In contrast, minimum player salaries, meal money, playoff pay, pensions, and other compensation issues are negotiated by the unions for all players.

There are two additional participants shown in figure 1.1 who may become involved in the collective bargaining process: mediators and arbitrators. These are neutrals who assist in the resolution of disputes, either negotiation impasses or grievances. Until recently, many of the battles between management and labor in sports have been fought in the courts. As labor relations in sports evolves and becomes more mature, third-party neutrals are taking on a more varied and important role than in the past.

Collective Bargaining

National Labor Relations Act

Workers involved in interstate commerce, which includes professional team sports, are covered by the National Labor Relations Act (NLRA), as amended.[9] Section 7 of this law provides three basic rights that form the heart of labor relations policy in the United States: (1) the right to self-organization, to form, join, or assist labor organizations; (2) the right to bargain collectively through representatives of their own choosing; and (3) the right to engage in "concerted activities" for employees' mutual aid or protection. In short, workers are permitted to unionize, collectively bargain, and use pressure tactics (e.g., strike and picket) to achieve their legitimate objectives. Administration is carried out by the National Labor Relations Board (NLRB) and the federal courts.

The NLRB enforces the law by policing unfair labor practices committed by either labor or management. For example, the employer and union are forbidden from interfering with employees' rights under section 7, and allegations of such violations are handled by the NLRB. Also administered by the NLRB is a machinery for determining appropriate units or groups of employees qualified to vote in a union representation election and for conducting such elections by secret ballot vote. Finally, the NLRB reviews questions concerning what issues are subject to negotiation under the law. The NLRB is not currently active in the administration of unit determination and elections in the major sports, although it may become so if a new league is formed. Units include active players, and elections involving players have resulted in the choice of an exclusive bargaining agency. Most of the NLRB's current work in sports involves unfair labor practices and scope of bargaining.

On unfair labor practices, two common allegations in sports are that the employer has disciplined or discharged players for engaging in union activities, and that the employer has refused to bargain in "good faith." Good faith bargaining requires that the parties communicate through proposals and counterproposals and that they make every reasonable effort to reach agreement. In certain cases, employers must furnish basic information about finances and budgets in order to comply with good faith dictates. There has been recurring conflict over this issue in sports, since owners are reluctant to disclose financial data to unions.

The scope of bargaining is defined in the NLRA as including wages, hours, and working conditions. Wages include pay, fringe benefits, and bonus payments; hours refer to time spent on the job; and working conditions are factors influencing the work environment, such as work rules, safety, and seniority. These topics are considered by the NLRB to be mandatory subjects for bargaining that must be negotiated in good faith. So-called permissive subjects for bargaining are those on which management is not obligated to negotiate but may do so if it wishes. This includes management rights or prerogatives that the employer has an exclusive right to determine. Illegal subjects are those the law prohibits from being negotiated. From time to time, the NLRB has been asked to rule in a sports industry case on whether a subject, such as wage scales or use of artificial turf, is negotiable.

Introduction

The Structure of Bargaining

The characteristics of bargaining units are generally the same throughout the team sports. All active league players are in the unit, and nearly all players are members of their respective unions. Clubs join together in bargaining with unions, so that the negotiated contract in each sport applies to all teams uniformly. The formal bargaining structure influences the diversity of individual and organizational interests that must be accommodated during the negotiation of an agreement. Conflict is inherent in nearly all negotiating situations, both between the parties and within the union or team management.

For most private industry and public employment, bargaining is limited to a single union dealing with a single firm or government employer. In several industries, however, contracts are negotiated on a national basis, applying to employees throughout the country. Because of the weakening of some firms in major American industries, the traditional style of pattern bargaining—in which agreements reached with a target firm have a substantial influence on agreements reached by the same union with other firms in the industry—is becoming less important. In the United States about one-sixth of all collective bargaining agreements are negotiated by associations of private employers.[10] Multiemployer bargaining is found in the lumber, coal, construction, longshoring, railroad, trucking, hotel, and retail grocery industries. It is also found in professional sports, where individual teams band together through the league format to negotiate a contract with the players' union that applies equally to all teams. The agreements reached in professional sports are not industrywide, however, because each of the sports has a separate contract with unions. Another feature that makes sports unique is the multilateral nature of bargaining. The clubs bargain as a group with unions over certain aspects of wages, hours, and working conditions, but the most important issue—individual salary—is negotiated between the club and player. The significance of this distinctive element of the structure of sports bargaining will be evident in several examples offered in later chapters to illustrate the dynamics of the process. Unions have been actively involved in clearing the way for greater labor market freedom for players to negotiate individual contracts, but their role is indirect in the sense that they are not responsible for reaching agreement on individual salaries.

Jack Barbash calls bargaining a "love-hate," "cooperation-conflict" relationship.[11] The parties realize their common interest in maximizing the income that finances their respective shares. But conflict arises over division of the economic pie. Most American managers and union leaders, and particularly in professional sports, view negotiations as a contest in which the "smart player" wins. Negotiation *strategy* is the overall plan of how to proceed at the bargaining table—at one pole is taking the "hard line," while at the other end is cooperating. *Tactics* are the specific methods that a party uses to implement its strategy, for example, adopting unrealistic positions, trading off issues, or such pressure tactics as strikes and lockouts. The adversarial strategy thus sets the tone for the labor-management relationship and the kinds of tactics that are employed.

Tactically, both sides usually adopt extreme positions. The union has its "shopping list," in which it asks for gains on many issues far beyond what it thinks realistically possible. Management typically offers very little at the outset. Both parties recognize the need to bluff and make dire threats with no real intention of carrying them out. Although the union is ordinarily the moving party in making demands at the outset of negotiations, an effective position for management is making high, hard demands of its own at the outset. Underlying this tactic is the adage that the best defense is a good offense. In recent years, throughout American industry and increasingly in professional sports, management has been trying to get unions to accept give-backs that reduce benefits gained under the previous contract. This tactic has been generally successful in much of U.S. industry, but has not produced significant retrenchment in sports so far. Negotiators are keenly aware of the fact that they must ultimately secure the approval of their principals for whatever they tentatively agree on. Rejections create serious problems for both parties, who must then return to the bargaining table for further efforts at shaping acceptable compromise.

Contents of Agreements

Typical collective bargaining agreements contain many pages of legalistic language spelling out the formal relationship between the parties. Key areas of these agreements include:

1. Specification of contract length. The duration is usually from one to five years, with three years most common. There may be provision for reopening the contract during its life for renegotiation of certain issues.

2. Compensation, which includes wages, pensions, and other fringe benefits. In sports, there are several areas of individual compensation that are not covered in the negotiated agreement. Unions in sports negotiate the minimum standards, but supplements to the minimum are covered in the individual bargaining process.

3. Rules for the utilization of labor, such as length of the workday, work practices, overtime, and health and safety. In sports, the big issue is free agency for players, which allows them to move liberally among teams to command greater individual bargaining power.

4. Individual job rights in such areas as seniority and discipline. Concern in sports has centered on discipline for aberrant behavior such as violence, gambling, and drug abuse.

5. Rights of union and management in the bargaining relationship, such as a management rights clause and provision for union security (e.g., union shop, dues checkoff). The prevailing practice in sports is for negotiation of an agency shop. This requires players who elect not to join the union to pay a service fee to the union (usually the equivalent of union dues) for its bargaining, legal, and grievance handling services.

6. Methods for enforcing, interpreting, and administering the agreement terms on a day-to-day basis: for example, grievance procedures, grievance arbitration, and no-strike clauses.

The provisions of a collective bargaining agreement are applied to situations that arise in the employment relationship. Management and union representatives may differ in the meaning they attach to a particular contract clause. The typical pattern is for management to act on its interpretation. Then, if the union objects to management's action, a grievance will be filed and may later be decided by an arbitrator. These actions and reactions give vitality to the language of the agreement throughout its duration.

2. Baseball

There is a lively debate among sports historians as to when baseball began and who invented it. Ball games, including the British game of rounders, were played with bats, balls, pitchers, and four bases in the early nineteenth century in New York and New England. The individual who first codified the rules of baseball, roughly as they are today, was Alexander Joy Cartwright. Much of the credit for invention of the game, however, is given to Abner Doubleday, who later became a U.S. Army major general in the Civil War. According to legend, Doubleday handed down the rules and laid out the first baseball diamond at Cooperstown, New York, in 1839. But this was several years after Cartwright's rules and the real beginnings of the game.

Baseball is the oldest major professional sport in America. The National League was formed in 1876 and the American League in 1899. Baseball is also the first sport in which a union broke through to achieve significant gains for players. As such, it has had a great influence on the collective bargaining models that have emerged in football, basketball, and hockey. Until recently, however, the union representing players in major league baseball was relatively weak compared to the owners. Monopolistic control by owners over salaries and the labor market gave the union little room to maneuver. But arbitration and court decisions in the mid-1970s dramatically shifted the balance of power toward the players. These changes are still stimulating player salaries, so that in addition to the power structure, the economics of baseball have been radically altered.

Economics of Baseball

In the business of baseball, as in other professional sports, the product is the game itself, presented by players as entertainment. This entertainment is consumed by the public through live viewing or, more commonly, through the print media, radio, and television. Economic rewards to clubs and players alike are directly related to success at the box office and with television contracts. But in baseball myriad other factors additionally motivate economic behavior.[1]

Table 2.1 shows the sources of revenues and expenses for major league teams in 1984. The data represent no team in particular, but rather give the lowest and highest revenues and expenditures among the teams in general. There is substantial variation in individual items. Although national television revenues are equal for all teams, income from ticket sales, local media broadcasting, and concessions and parking show a wide disparity. Expenses also vary widely, with some teams spending nearly four times as much on player salaries than others. In 1984 and 1985, according to various estimates, seventeen to twenty-two teams were at the break-even point or were losing money. While it is clear that baseball franchises are not as profitable as they were before free agency, reports that the baseball business is in deplorable shape are somewhat exaggerated. Tax advantages to clubs, such as depreciation of players, can turn what appears to be a loss into a profit, and reports of player salaries can be deceptive, since some of the payments to players are deferred and do not involve immediate out-of-pocket costs to clubs. A detailed picture of the economics of baseball is difficult to draw because clubs do not reveal their books and accounting practices to the public.

Monopoly Control

Baseball leagues constitute a cartel or self-regulating monopoly. This monopoly control is the cornerstone on which the industry is based and influences its economic rewards. The leagues are subject to some control from the outside by the government; however, this regulation is far less burden-

Table 2.1   Range of Revenues and Expenses in Team Operations, 1984 (in millions)

Revenues

Ticket sales	$4.0–15.0
National television	4.0
Local television, radio	1.4–11.7
Concessions, parking	0.4–5.0
Miscellaneous[a]	2.0
Total revenues	11.8–37.7

Expenses

Payroll	$4.0–15.0
Minor league system	2.0–4.5
Scouting	0.75–3.00
General and administrative	1.5–3.0
Marketing	0.3–2.0
Stadium rent	0–2.0
Team support[b]	0.7–1.0
Total expenses	9.25–30.5

Source: Data from estimates by team executives, and based in part on Glenn Kramon, "A Hard Look: No Fun at the Old Ballpark," *San Francisco Sunday Examiner and Chronicle* , 7 October 1984, A-1.

Notes: a. Includes royalties and sponsorships.
    b. Includes travel, per diem, and medical.

some than it is for other monopolistic industries, such as public utilities. Internal control in baseball is effected by the players' union, and the contest for economic power in the industry is between management and labor. Yet the union has only nominal, if any, influence on the arrangements between owners on matters of mutual interest, such as scheduling games, advertising, promotion of the game, rules, expansion of teams, and drafting of players. This is consistent with the management rights or prerogatives that employers have in industries outside sport. The important difference is that, because of an antitrust exemption that the industry enjoys, baseball owners can engage in noncompetitive arrangements to collude, fix prices, and restrain trade.

When artificial barriers are erected, the normal checks and balances of the market and free enterprise systems are not allowed to operate. The operation of the baseball cartel cuts two ways. Suppose, for example, that players had complete freedom to move in the labor market. This would probably escalate salaries to far higher levels than they are now, and could do serious damage to the continuity of teams that spark fan loyalty. On the other hand, the restraint of trade that owners carry out through the league cartel has the potential for public harm in that people wind up paying a higher price for the entertainment.[2] The saving grace for baseball is that ticket prices are still a relative bargain because of high stadium capacities and the relatively large number of games played by teams. Moreover, many games are televised free for viewers. Therefore, because baseball entertainment is available to the public in relative abundance and at low prices, government regulators have been wary of interfering with the operation of the industry.

Tax Advantages

A primary attraction to ownership of a professional team in baseball, as well as other sports, is the advantage of low-tax operation. Businesses in general are allowed to depreciate their assets under rules of the Internal Revenue Code. If a tractor, building, or computer is purchased, it can be depreciated or deducted from revenues under the rationale that it gets used up or wears out. As a deducted cost of doing business, depreciation reduces taxes. Only sports businesses are allowed to depreciate their human assets. Player contracts are purchased by owners, in transactions separate from the purchase of the franchise, and then players are written off as depreciable assets in from three to seven years. The franchise, or right of ownership, itself is a nondepreciable asset. It therefore makes sense to assign a low value to the franchise for tax purposes and a high value to the players' contracts so that depreciation can be maximized. Despite some tightening of depreciation rules in sports in recent years, allowing no more than 50 percent of the acquisition price of a club to be written off in player depreciation, ownership of teams remains a lucrative tax haven.

Another tax advantage available to many baseball owners is free or low rent of stadium facilities. Communities anxious to lure or retain major league franchises are willing to give tax breaks that are in effect underwritten by the citizens. This taxpayer subsidization is not unjustified because teams generate substantial revenues from parking, food and beverage service, and souvenir stands. The games attract tourists who patronize local business establishments. Moreover, the image of a community is enhanced by having a major league baseball team.

Attendance and Television

Despite the strike in 1981 that interrupted play and cut attendance sharply, in 1982 and 1983 major league baseball set new gate records. In 1983 about 45.5 million persons came to the ball parks, an increase of about 2 percent over 1982. Because ticket prices were raised by nearly 9 percent on the average (to about $5), total revenues from attendance rose by about 11.5 percent.[3] In 1984 attendance fell to 44.7 million, although it was still 50 percent higher than in 1975.

These increases reflect a growing popularity of baseball, spurred by widening the base of interest through geographic expansion of markets and contemporary methods of marketing and promotion. Free agency has helped to balance the talent among clubs and raise new hopes for fans. The close pennant races of the 1982, 1983, and 1985 seasons were also important factors in sustaining interest, and the decline in attendance in 1984 was due to the fact that only one of the four division races was closely contested.

Apart from attendance, the other big source of revenue to baseball teams is national and local television. Television revenues show healthy economic growth. Major league baseball's national television agreement with ABC and NBC, covering the six-year period from 1984 through 1989, provides a total revenue package of $1.125 billion. This revenue raises the amount received by nearly four times over the old national television contract.

Local television agreements are also negotiated by clubs. These provide additional revenues depending on the size of the market. The Atlanta Braves' games are broadcast throughout the nation by owner Ted Turner's cable television network. In 1985, at the urging of Commissioner Ueberroth, Turner agreed to pay nearly $30 million to major league baseball over five years in return for no restriction on the number of games that he can telecast. Although several local television contracts are with local or regional stations and provide free entertainment to viewers, the trend is toward cable television, which charges a fee for its service. Local television creates large disparities in potential revenue to clubs, with New York, Los Angeles, and

Chicago able to generate far greater amounts than clubs in Minnesota, Seattle, and Pittsburgh. This causes teams with extensive market areas to be able to attract higher quality players with bigger salaries. As pay television expands, the gap between rich and poor markets will widen.

A possible solution to the rich-get-richer problem of local market disparity is to share these television revenues the way teams do under the national contracts. Teams in rich markets, however, have no incentive to divide this wealth. Prevention of excessive dominance by the rich teams at the expense of the poor ones may eventually find its solution in government regulation requiring revenue sharing. Should this occur or some means for sharing be voluntarily adopted by owners, it would probably be well into the future. However this may unfold, it is clear that the growing attendance and fat television arrangements are an incentive to players to try to get a bigger piece of the revenue pie.

Structure of Employment

Professional baseball is covered by the National Labor Relations Act. While the National Labor Relations Board has the statutory power to decline jurisdiction if the influence of an industry on commerce does not warrant it, it has ruled that baseball is subject to its jurisdiction.[4] The antitrust laws, on the other hand, have not been found to extend to baseball because of a 1922 U.S. Supreme Court decision.[5] The Court, in an opinion written by Justice Oliver Wendell Holmes, ruled that playing exhibition games was not within interstate commerce. This exemption from the antitrust laws is unique to baseball. It does not apply to football, basketball, or hockey.

The absence of antitrust law regulation enabled owners to maintain full control over the market through their exclusive rights to bargain with players allocated to them. If a player sought to challenge the reserve clause, the courts, citing the 1922 decision, would find for the club. For instance, in a case involving player Curt Flood, the Supreme Court refused to go against a half century of precedent by overruling the 1922 case, despite Flood's claim that the reserve clause was illegal and severely reduced player salaries.[6] The Court based its decision on its recognition and acceptance of baseball's unique characteristics and needs. The antitrust exemption continues to apply formally to baseball, but it has come under closer scrutiny in recent years. For example, the joint Senate-House Committee on Professional Sports in 1977 stated that there is no justification for baseball's immunity from the antitrust laws and recommended that Congress remove the exemption. That Congress has not taken action on baseball's antitrust immunity is mostly due to the fact that the players' union has been able to achieve greater leverage with management than it had in the past. This makes the exemption for baseball a less onerous burden for today's players.

Management

It is customary to think of management in terms of individual owners because of their visibility in the media which portray such flamboyant owners as Ted Turner of the Atlanta Braves and George Steinbrenner of the New York Yankees as modern captains of industry with unquestioned control over operations. Although owners do exercise substantial domination of the internal management and finances of their teams, much of the labor relations is conducted through the league, where authority is shared. Baseball owners and their outside interests are shown in table 2.2.

The National and American Leagues of Professional Baseball Clubs are jointly responsible for two of the most important functions affecting industrial relations: collective bargaining and selection of the commissioner of baseball. Owners of the twenty-six teams have equal votes in these determinations, but they are subordinate to the will of the leagues under consensus management. In effect, the league is a cooperative pool or cartel. If its power is unchecked by a union or by government regulation, it can exercise exclusive control over labor markets. As a result, players can be paid far less than they would be worth under competitive circumstances. In response to this monopoly power, players have unionized and government has exercised a sharper oversight in its regulation of baseball.

Collective bargaining for the leagues is conducted by the Player Relations Committee (PRC), which is selected by the owners. The director of this committee is the chief negotiator. The 1973 and 1976 basic agreements in baseball were negotiated by John J. Gaherin. He was replaced by Raymond Grebey who handled the negotiations of 1980 and 1981. Grebey resigned in 1983 under pressure from the owners and was replaced by Lee MacPhail. Grebey's abrasive style in negotiations had not been successful, so the owners chose a more moderate representative. In his former position as presi-

---

Table 2.2   Ownership of Major League Baseball Franchises

American League	Principal Owners	What They Do
Baltimore Orioles	Edward Bennett Williams	Washington attorney
Boston Red Sox	Jean R. Yawkey Haywood C. Sullivan	Yawkey's late husband owned the Red Sox for 45 years; Sullivan was his longtime employee
California Angels	Gene Autry	Retired movie cowboy and former TV station owner
Chicago White Sox	Jerry M. Reinsdorf Edward M. Einhorn	Reinsdorf runs Balcor/American Express Realty; Einhorn is an ex-TV executive
Cleveland Indians	Estate of Francis J. O'Neill in trust for Catholic Charities Corp. of Cleveland	O'Neill was CEO of Leaseway Transportation
Detroit Tigers	Thomas S. Monaghan	President of Domino's Pizza Inc.
Kansas City Royals	Ewing Kauffman Avron B. Fogelman	Kauffman runs Marion Labs; Fogelman is a Memphis realtor
Milwaukee Brewers	Allan H. Selig and others	Selig is a Chevrolet dealer
Minnesota Twins	Carl R. Pohlad	President of Marquette Bank, Minneapolis
New York Yankees	George M. Steinbrenner III	CEO of American Shipbuilding Co.
Oakland Athletics	Walter A. Haas Jr.	Chairman, executive committee of Levi Strauss & Co.
Seattle Mariners	George L. Argyros	Owns Air California, real estate
Texas Rangers	Eddie Chiles	Chairman, Western Co. of North America (oil-field services)
Toronto Blue Jays	John Labatt Ltd. R. Howard Webster	Labatt is a beer and food conglomerate; Webster is a wealthy private investor
National League		
Atlanta Braves	Ted Turner	Owns a TV broadcasting station and cable services
Chicago Cubs	Tribune Co.	Newspapers, TV, and radio stations
Cincinnati Reds	Marge Schott	Chevrolet and Buick dealer
Houston Astros	John J. McMullen	Shipping magnate
Los Angeles Dodgers	Peter O'Malley	His major business is the Dodgers
Montreal Expos	Charles R. Bronfman	Deputy chairman and major shareholder, Seagram Co.
New York Mets	Nelson Doubleday	President and CEO, Doubleday & Co.
Philadelphia Phillies	Taft Broadcasting Co.	TV and radio stations, cable TV
Pittsburgh Pirates	City of Pittsburgh and several private investors	City government; private investments
St. Louis Cardinals	Anheuser-Busch Cos.	Breweries and bakeries
San Diego Padres	Joan Kroc	Her late husband founded McDonald's Corp.
San Francisco Giants	Bob Lurie	Owns Lurie Co., a real estate business

Source: *Business Week*, 12 August 1985, 43, as updated by author.

dent of the American League, MacPhail had considerable experience at the bargaining table as a member of the management team, and his relations with the union have been generally good. His capable leadership helped limit the duration of the 1985 players strike.

The Commissioner

Baseball's first commissioner was Kenesaw Mountain Landis, a dominating figure and former federal court judge, who was hired in 1921 to restore sanctity and banish from baseball the "Black Sox" players who fixed the 1919 World Series. His successors, Albert ("Happy") Chandler, Ford Frick, and General William D. Eckert, were uninspiring leaders who seemed unable to act decisively. In 1969 the owners elevated the National League's attorney, Bowie Kuhn, to the job of commissioner. Kuhn's tenure was controversial among the owners, but he brought an enlightened and spirited leadership to the position. He overturned player trades by Charles O. Finley, owner of the Oakland A's, in the "interests of baseball"; fined San Diego Padre owner Ray Kroc $100,000 for tampering; and banned retired player Willie Mays from participation as an official in baseball because of his business relations with an Atlantic City casino. Over the years Kuhn had to slap the hands of numerous owners, which built up animosity and resistance to his continuing as commissioner. Yet he presided over unprecedented prosperity for the game. His apparent indecisiveness over the 1981 baseball strike was the result of his job description, not his leadership ability.

Kuhn needed approval of three-fourths of the owners in each league to win another term in office. A disgruntled minority of the owners finally managed to force him out, but he was retained in a lame duck capacity through the 1984 season when his successor, Peter Ueberroth, who achieved national prominence as head of the Los Angeles Olympic Organizing Committee, took over.

Before taking the job of baseball commissioner, Ueberroth, in consultation with Kuhn, who really designed the changes to be proposed to management, was able to get the owners to accept a considerable strengthening of the position. The most important change, and one which has already had a significant effect on industrial relations, is that the commissioner is formally recognized as baseball's chief executive officer and all departments report directly to him. This allows the commissioner to exercise a more decisive role in the collective bargaining process. He does not actually participate in the negotiations, but acts more like the president of a company, with power to determine, ratify, and reject arrangements that are made by management representatives at the bargaining table.

Another important change in the rules affecting the operation of the commissioner's office is that he needs approval of only a majority vote of the twenty-six teams for reelection, with a minimum of five votes from each league. Had such a rule existed before, Kuhn would have been able to remain in office. Also, the commissioner is empowered to fine teams a maximum of $250,000. This strengthening of the office gives Ueberroth greater freedom to act than any commissioner since Judge Landis.

Labor

The Major League Baseball Players Association (MLBPA) was formed in 1952. Like its predecessor, the American Baseball Guild, the association was initially dominated by the team owners. Negotiated agreements were reached on a limited number of issues such as pensions and insurance. But in 1966, Marvin Miller was hired as the MLBPA executive director. Miller took a more traditional trade union stance with the club owners, and in 1968 negotiated an agreement on a broad range of issues.[7]

Then, in the 1970 agreement, the MLBPA negotiated a significant breakthrough, a provision for a tripartite grievance arbitration panel with a permanent impartial chairman. This replaced a system under which disputes over the interpretation of the collective bargaining agreement were finally ruled on by the commissioner of baseball.

The more forceful posture of the players' union became apparent in 1972 when the season was delayed ten days as a result of a strike. In the ensuing 1973 agreement, another key change was negotiated by the union. This was a clause providing for determination of players' salaries by neutral arbitrators, if the player and club were unable to come to terms.

When the 1973 collective bargaining agreement expired on December 31, 1975, the parties were unable to come to terms on a replacement until July 1976 (the agreement was made retroactive to January 1). The new contract, in effect through the end of 1979, continued grievance and salary arbitration. An important new provision revised the reserve clause, which previously tied a player to a particular team. Players were thus permitted, under certain conditions, to become free agents, selling their services to the highest bidder.

These accomplishments by the MLBPA established the modern era in labor relations that has affected all professional team sports. Especially important are the use of grievance arbitration for contract interpretation disputes, salary arbitration, and rules regulating free agency. Each of these collective bargaining agreement provisions was the brainchild of Marvin Miller.[8] A former assistant to the president of the United Steelworkers of America, Miller was known as a creative thinker and had experience as a negotiator before he became executive director of the MLBPA. He took a weak, owner-dominated union and fused its membership into a united front. He not only excelled in winning unprecedented gains at the bargaining table, but managed to preserve those gains from later attack by management. Reggie Jackson and Tom Seaver are among the prominent players who assisted Miller as team representatives during the years in which important breakthroughs were made in collective bargaining.

In 1982 the aging Miller announced his intention to retire as MLBPA executive director. He was replaced by Kenneth Moffett, who as acting director of the Federal Mediation and Conciliation Service had played a peacemaker role during the baseball strike of 1981. The choice seemed a good one, particularly in light of the changing of the guard on the management side. Miller and Ray Grebey were old antagonists. With them guiding the bargaining, future strike possibilities loomed large. Fresh leadership would help the parties move toward a more cooperative relationship that would help ensure labor peace.

About a year after his appointment, however, Moffett was fired by the MLBPA's executive board, ostensibly for his lack of militancy toward management.[9] The MLBPA denied that Miller had anything to do with the decision to fire Moffett. But Moffett believed that Miller orchestrated his ouster.[10] Whatever the case, one matter that created controversy within the union was Moffett's stand on drug abuse. He was a key member of a joint labor-management committee that was drafting guidelines for handling players who commit drug violations. Donald Fehr, the union's general counsel, and Mark Bellanger, Moffett's assistant, opposed Moffett's view that the union should participate in disciplining players for drug abuse. Fehr and Bellanger did not want the union to have a disciplinary role because they preferred to work out problems through the grievance procedure. Their position was consistent with the adage "management acts, and the union reacts," which describes traditional labor relations. Whether a more proactive role by the MLBPA was a wise solution to a problem that affects both players and management was uncertain at the time, especially since the magnitude of the drug problem had not come to full light. Since, however, there had been little joint problem solving in baseball and traditional models had not worked out successfully, it might well have been beneficial to adopt a more cooperative approach.

When Moffett was fired, Miller resumed leadership of the union on an interim basis. His eventual replacement was Donald Fehr, with whom Miller had worked closely for several years. As executive director, Fehr is somewhat more subdued than Miller, but his tough stance during the 1985 negotiations and his resistance to mandatory drug testing indicate that he adheres closely to Miller's style of leadership. Miller has continued to influence policy, although his nearly legendary work pace was slowed by a heart attack in 1985.

Moffett became assistant to the president of another union, the National Association of Broadcast Engineers and Technicians. He has come out of his brief episode as head of the MLBPA looking good. Moffett's efforts to rid baseball of its drug problems were well intentioned and on the right course. Although he did not participate in later drug control initiatives, his ideas influenced the policy changes. Moffett also was vindicated for his 1984 revelation that Keith Hernandez of the New York Mets was involved in an FBI drug investigation. At the time, Hernandez flatly denied ever having used cocaine and threatened to sue Moffett unless he apologized. When Hernandez's cocaine use came to light in the 1985 Pittsburgh drug hearings, he publicly apologized to Moffett in a turnaround that was fraught with irony.

Strike of 1981

The strike is the players' ultimate weapon for achieving negotiation objectives. Because of the multiemployer bargaining structure in baseball, a strike affects all teams in the league. Once playing dates are lost they are difficult, if not impossible, to make up later. A shutdown in the games affects numerous other businesses that derive their revenues in whole or in part from baseball. Television loses a major attraction; concession stands close;

and airlines, hotels, restaurants, and bars lose their baseball fan clientele. Before 1981 there had been brief strikes in baseball, but none had a significant effect on regular season play. Players struck in 1972 over a pension dispute, but the strike resulted in the cancellation of only eighty-six games. In 1976 the owners shut down training camps for seventeen days as a result of an impasse in bargaining over free agency.

Negotiations that ultimately led to the 1981 strike began the previous year with an attempt to reach a new collective bargaining agreement. Under the old agreement the players had solidified their rights to achieve free agency, and the owners were trying to regain greater controls over player mobility. The crux of the dispute was compensation for clubs that lost free agents. The owners reasoned that if they could require teams that signed free agents to compensate teams that lost them by replacement with a good player, this would put a crimp on free agency and moderate the salary escalation.

A strike appeared imminent before the start of the 1980 season but was headed off when the parties agreed to separate free agency compensation from other bargaining issues. A committee with management and union representatives was created to study free agency. Although an agreement was reached on the other issues, the study committee was unable to resolve the free agency issue. When the owners indicated their intention to put their own compensation plan for free agents into effect, the players announced their intention to strike on May 29, 1981. Meanwhile, the NLRB intervened when the union filed an unfair labor practice charge maintaining that the owners' refusal to disclose financial data was a refusal to bargain in good faith. But when the NLRB went to U.S. district court to try to get an injunction to postpone the strike for another year, the court refused to grant it.

Because of the legal wrangling to avert the strike its commencement was delayed until June 12. The owners sought to minimize the effect by purchasing $50 million in strike insurance from Lloyd's of London and by creating a $15 million strike fund from owner contributions in the previous two years. The players, on the other hand, had no previously planned insulation from the financial impact of the strike. They relied on player solidarity within their union to make the strike successful. The owners hoped that as the strike went on and the players realized how much they were losing in forgone salaries, they would start warring among themselves. But the players stuck together.

A notable feature of the bargaining that went on during the strike was the acrimonious relationship between union leader Marvin Miller and the owners' chief negotiator, Ray Grebey. They exchanged sharp verbal attacks in the media regularly, which only served to make compromise difficult and prolong the strike. Mediation was attempted by Kenneth Moffett of the Federal Mediation and Conciliation Service, but he made little progress in bringing the hostile negotiators to common ground. What finally created pressure to end the strike was fear that the entire baseball season would be lost.

The strike resulted in the cancellation of 713 games. The strike ended after fifty days when both sides made substantial compromise. Free agency compensation rules were tightened, but the players retained the right to move to other clubs without much market restraint. In effect, the players won the strike because their salaries continued to increase rapidly.

Attendance and television ratings flagged after the strike, as many fans lost interest in the truncated season. But fears that the strike would do permanent damage to fan interest proved unfounded. With a fresh start in the new season of 1982, attendance reached record levels and the strike faded into history. It is clear that owners, players, and fans all suffered from the strike, and the fact that it occurred became a moderating force against having another strike, especially a long one, in the future.

Player Salaries

Salary Trends

The MLBPA negotiates minimum player salaries and the maximum amount that salaries can be reduced from one year to the next (no more than 20 percent of the previous year or in excess of 30 percent of the salary two years previous). Otherwise, salaries are negotiated by the individual players, often through agents, and team management. The player seeks a salary that is more than adequate to provide sufficient income in his productive years in the game. To most players and their agents, this means the maximum amount obtainable. Although many former players get high-paying jobs in a second career because of their earlier sports affiliation, they try to offset in present salaries the future negative effects on income caused by loss of experience in the nonsport job market.

As shown in table 2.3 average salaries in baseball have increased dramatically, especially since 1976. The rising salaries in baseball, which reached an average of $371,000 in 1985, do not appear to reflect qualitative differences in the players. Expansion of the major leagues has brought in a far larger number of players than would have qualified in earlier times. Along with economic factors such as tax advantages to owners, rising attendance, and lucrative television contracts for the clubs, collective bargaining has been a crucial factor in the salary increases. The opportunity to achieve free agency status, won by the union, has been especially important. Also contributing to the salary increases is the availability of arbitration for determining individual player salaries. What is of primary interest is the magnitude and growth of salaries and the relative salaries of players according to position and team.

Table 2.3   Major League Baseball Salaries, 1970–85

Year	Minimum Salary	Average Salary	Percent Change
1970	$12,000	$ 29,303	—
1971	12,750	31,543	7.6
1972	13,500	34,092	8.1
1973	15,000	36,566	7.3
1974	15,000	40,839	11.7
1975	16,000	44,676	9.4
1976	19,000	51,501	15.3
1977	19,000	76,066	47.7
1978	21,000	99,876	31.3
1979	21,000	113,558*	13.7
1980	30,000	143,756*	26.6
1981	32,500	185,651*	29.1
1982	33,500	241,497*	30.1
1983	35,000	289,194*	19.8
1984	40,000	329,408*	14.1
1985	40,000	371,157	12.7

Source: Major League Baseball Players Association.

Note: *Salary figures have been discounted for salary deferrals without interest at a rate of 9 percent per year for the period of delayed payments.

Baseball

A look at average salaries by player position (see table 2.4) shows that third basemen were the highest paid in 1985, at about $602,000. Data on average salary by position for a given year should be interpreted with caution because they tend to fluctuate annually with the rise to prominence of exceptional players and the retirement or change in position played by other exceptional players. For example, in 1983 the highest paid position was designated hitter, which was at the time a position dominated by some of the heaviest hitting and therefore highest paid players in the game. On the other hand, in 1985 there was a large number of remarkably talented third basemen (e.g., Mike Schmidt, George Brett, Wade Boggs, and Bob Horner), whose salary increases raised the average pay for that category. Unlike average salaries for quarterbacks in football and centers in basketball, which are generally the highest compensated positions in those sports, baseball data show greater variation by position from year to year. It should also be noted that the data in table 2.4 represent only a portion of the regular players at each position, and thus not all players in the major leagues. Therefore, the average salaries shown are higher than the overall average salary data in table 2.3 would suggest.

Apart from such circumstances as position, overall wealth of the owner, access to free agency, and salary arbitration, several performance factors are important in determining an individual player's salary. One is hitting or

Table 2.4   Average Salaries in Baseball, by Position, 1985

Position	Number of Players	Average Salary
First base	22	$525,145
Second base	23	379,998
Third base	23	601,595
Shortstop	21	434,425
Outfield	68	468,985
Catcher	21	452,803
Designated hitter	13	447,334
Starting pitcher	109	397,730
Relief pitcher	101	312,313

Source: Major League Baseball Players Association.

pitching performance, measured by various comparative statistical categories. Another is the weight of the player's contribution to team performance, which is more difficult to measure accurately. Number of years in the major leagues carries weight as a seniority and fan recognition factor. Also, acknowledged star or superstar players, whose charisma or clutch performances stand out, command higher salaries.[11] Agents compile computerized information on the players they represent, as well as on comparable players, for use in salary negotiations and arbitrations with owners.

There is a strong correlation between pay and performance. Table 2.5 shows the average baseball salaries by team from 1980 to 1984. There is a positive correlation between high salaries and winning teams. A common

Table 2.5   Average Baseball Team Salaries, 1980–84

Salary Ranking	1984	1983	1982	1981	1980
1. New York Yankees	$458,544	$463,687	$411,988	$309,855	$242,937
2. Chicago White Sox	447,281	291,114	247,673	192,658	72,415
3. California	431,431	389,833	423,403	259,404	191,014
4. Chicago Cubs	422,194	268,947	220,662	125,117	160,209
5. Atlanta	402,689	347,620	209,492	195,449	147,989
6. Philadelphia	401,476	442,165	390,370	289,971	221,274
7. Milwaukee	385,215	352,061	330,965	243,882	159,086
8. Oakland	384,027	266,815	266,335	148,065	54,994
9. Houston	382,991	364,825	306,565	260,789	176,720
10. Detroit	371,332	263,899	174,134	160,561	86,988
11. Montreal	368,557	353,357	299,192	195,958	158,196
12. Baltimore	360,204	305,305	242,558	169,919	116,156
13. Pittsburgh	330,661	314,769	251,234	206,359	199,185
14. Los Angeles	316,530	288,555	216,332	192,104	183,124
15. San Diego	311,199	261,820	137,946	103,106	138,978
16. Boston	297,878	264,883	247,513	223,252	184,686
17. Toronto	295,632	213,087	127,860	97,271	67,218
18. Kansas City	291,160	309,962	258,091	112,910	100,453
19. St. Louis	290,886	259,393	327,533	207,654	173,480
20. New York Mets	282,952	306,253	263,539	201,303	126,488
21. San Francisco	282,132	248,204	198,438	185,939	148,265
22. Cincinnati	269,019	239,068	203,532	201,557	162,655
23. Texas	247,081	180,848	186,424	178,131	148,792
24. Minnesota	172,024	97,980	67,335	85,736	80,358
25. Seattle	168,505	118,875	114,405	95,263	82,244
26. Cleveland	159,774	242,134	216,000	186,396	127,505

Source: Major League Baseball Players Association.

occurrence is that teams in low-population areas, such as Minnesota, sell, trade, or lose by free agency their good players to high-population areas like New York. The player is simply worth more to the richer teams than to the poorer ones because of demographics and local television revenues. Contrary to this pattern, however, the New York Yankees, the highest paying team with an average salary approaching a half-million dollars, did not make the playoffs from 1983 to 1985. Another exception, the Baltimore Orioles, the winner of the World Series in 1983, had only the eleventh highest average salary. The Orioles have generally avoided the free agency market and concentrated instead on developing young players in a strong farm system.[12] The Detroit Tigers and Kansas City Royals, who won the World Series in 1984 and 1985, have similar policies.

Deferred Compensation

Multimillion dollar contracts signed by baseball players have become commonplace in baseball. A large and growing number of players are reaping huge rewards for playing the game. However, these financial bonanzas are not always what they appear to be on the surface, because most of these contracts provide for some form of deferred compensation. Before 1976, multiyear contracts were very rare in baseball. With the signings of free agents under the new rules, teams tried to lock players into longer terms. Instead of receiving all the compensation up front or within a short period, payments may be spread out for ten, twenty, or more years.[13] Players ordinarily receive a guaranteed salary for the period of time that they play. The deferred payments usually start after the player retires from the game. Annual salaries involve direct out-of-pocket costs to the club, but if payments are deferred, the cost to the club is reduced significantly.

Suppose, for example, that a player signs a "million-dollar" contract providing $100,000 a year spread over ten years. If the team invests the million dollars at a 10 percent return, the player would still receive a million dollars, but the actual cost to the team is reduced dramatically by deferring payments to the player and securing returns from investing the balance of the million dollars.

Teams with strong financial positions may opt for high-return investments to fund amounts due players under deferred contracts. Less financially capable teams may use their available funds to keep afloat; therefore they too prefer deferred payments. Apart from helping their cash flow, these teams are in effect mortgaging the future in hope that operating revenues in years to come will cover their contractual debts. Of course, the risk involved for the player who signs a deferred compensation contract without guarantee is that the corporation or person who owns the team will go bankrupt.

The benefits of deferred compensation are not one-sided. Not only do the teams gain, but so can the players. Deferred compensation is taxable in the year it is paid rather than the year it is committed. Assuming a maximum tax bracket for individuals of 50 percent, it may not be in the interest of a player to sign a contract that provides large amounts of income taxed at the maximum rate over a short period. By extending the payments under the contract, the player can receive money after his retirement from baseball, when he would probably be in a lower tax bracket. Also, many professional athletes have trouble hanging on to their money, so deferred payments represent a type of forced savings.

Apart from the potential inability of a team to make long-term payments because of insolvency, another risk for the player is inflation. If deferred payments are not protected against inflation, future compensation may be paid in far cheaper dollars. For this reason, more players are insisting on cost-of-living clauses in their contracts.

Free Agency

Under the reserve clause in baseball, when a player signs a contract he becomes the property of the club. If he is traded or put on waivers, the acquiring club obtains exclusive rights to him. Even if he retires and later decides to return to the game, he is bound to the last club with which he had a contract. Before its modification, the reserve clause was a disincentive for owners to pay high salaries to players. Nearly all contracts were for a single year, which gave players hardly any job or pay security. Bound to a single team, the player had no real alternative but to sign a contract for another year with that team, accepting what the owner was willing to pay. Once players signed a contract with a reserve clause, team owners had monopsony control— there was only one buyer of the player's services.

As a result of grievance arbitration cases in 1974 and 1975, and of negotiated agreements between the MLBPA and owners that followed in 1976 and 1981, the rules obligating a player to remain with a team were altered significantly, and free agency came into being for the first time in any professional sport.

A weakness in the enforcement of a player contract was initially exploited by pitcher Jim Hunter of the Oakland A's. Hunter had agreed with club owner Charles O. Finley that half his 1974 salary would be set aside in an insurance trust. In 1970 the MLBPA had negotiated a provision for grievance arbitration in the collective bargaining agreement with the leagues, so that when the dispute arose between Hunter and Finley over payments into the insurance trust, the matter was brought to arbitration. The chairman of the arbitration panel, Peter Seitz, ruled that Finley had not met the conditions of the agreement and declared Hunter a free agent. Although this decision did not deal directly with the reserve clause, it showed that arbitration gave added protection to players whose contracts were not properly followed. Hunter subsequently signed a five-year contract with the New York Yankees, and the Seitz decision was upheld in court.

In 1975, another ruling by arbitrator Seitz made a direct assault on the reserve clause. The case involved two pitchers, Andy Messersmith of the Los Angeles Dodgers and Dave McNally of the Baltimore Orioles. These players contended that since they had played with their clubs for one year without a contract, their employment status could not be further extended unilaterally by the clubs. Seitz agreed, declaring the players free agents. The owners promptly fired Seitz and appealed his decision to the federal courts, contending that he had exceeded his authority as an arbitrator by nullifying the reserve system. But the arbitration decision was upheld.

Because the reserve clause was overturned, the team owners were eager to regain at least some limitation on the players' right to become free agents. Thus, the owners sought and won a provision in the 1976 collective bargaining agreement with the MLBPA that players must have had at least six years of major league service before they could become free agents, and that the clubs would draft free agents in reverse order of team standings. Still, the bargaining power of the players remained far greater than it had been under the earlier reserve clause and before free agency.

At the start of the 1976 season, approximately one hundred fifty players were unsigned. Many were seeking to become free agents at the end of the season, so that they could sign a contract with the highest bidder. Contrary to predictions, however, most of these players signed contracts during the season. By the end of the 1976 season, twenty-four out of the six hundred players in the major leagues had become free agents. This led to a much-publicized financial bonanza for some players, who profited from a bidding war among clubs for their services. In 1977, three players received multi-year contracts for more than $2 million each. Most observers thought that the salaries in the second reentry draft would be moderated, yet several of the thirty-five free agents drafted in the 1978 season were able to get contracts that greatly exceeded the previous levels.

In the first and second reentry drafts, the two teams spending the most money for free agents were the New York Yankees and California Angels, both located in heavily populated areas. In a fifteen-month period, the Yankees spent an estimated $9 million for four free agents.[14] The Yankees were the major league champions in 1977, but the Angels had a mediocre year, largely due to injuries sustained by key free agent draftees.

Although the number of players opting for free agency has not changed significantly in ensuing years of the draft, their salaries have continued to escalate rapidly. In the 1979 draft, for example, twenty-three free agents contracted for an estimated total of $32 million. The largest single amount paid to a free agent up to that time was provided in the contract signed in 1980 by Dave Winfield with the New York Yankees. Winfield was to receive $22 million over the next ten years. Table 2.6 shows the guaranteed salaries and duration of contract obtained by ten of the players who were eligible for free agency in 1983. Half of these players signed contracts as free agents, and the other half elected to sign contracts with their previous teams. The data indicate that a player does not have to sign with another team as a free agent in order to secure a high contract, because the opportunity of signing with another club makes the present owner more willing to match the market. In 1984 one of the top free agents, Bruce Sutter, went to the Atlanta Braves for a six-year contract worth $10.1 million. The other leading free agent, Rick Sutcliffe, elected to re-sign with the Chicago Cubs under a $9.5 million five-year contract.

As a result of the fifty-day baseball strike of 1981 and subsequent collective bargaining agreement, management and the players negotiated changes in the rules for compensation of teams that lose free agents. They were changed again as a result of the 1985 players' strike. Before these changes, the only compensation required for signing a free agent under the 1976 agreement was giving up a choice in the amateur draft. Under the 1982 rules, free agents were ranked as either A or B players, depending on per-

Table 2.6   Contracts Signed by Free Agents and Potential Free Agents, 1983

Free Agents	Team	Years Duration	Amount	
Steve Garvey	San Diego	5	$6.6	million
Steve Kemp	N.Y. Yankees	5	5.45	million
Floyd Bannister	Chicago White Sox	5	4.79	million
Don Baylor	N.Y. Yankees	4	3.675	million
Omar Moreno	Houston	5	3.5	million
Potential Free Agents				
Carney Lansford	Oakland	5	$5.4	million
Len Barker	Atlanta	5	4.5	million
Jerry Reuss	Los Angeles	4	4.4	million
Bob Boone	California	3	2.75	million
Doug DeCinces	California	3	2.7	million

Source: Data from *Sporting News*, 7 February 1983, 31; and 28 November 1983, 56.

formance. Players rated in the top 20 percent at their position were rated A. Players in the top 21 to 30 percent were rated B. If a player had gone through the reentry draft before or had twelve years of major league service, he was exempt from the rankings.

If a team signed an A-rated free agent, it was required to compensate the team that lost the free agent with a roster player chosen from a pool of unprotected players (only twenty-four players could be protected by each team). In addition, the team that lost a free agent got an extra choice in the amateur draft. When a B-rated free agent was signed, the team that lost the player got two extra choices in the draft of amateur players. Up to five clubs were allowed to exempt themselves from contributing to the compensation pool by agreeing not to draft any A-rated players for three years. Five teams exercised this option in 1982: Los Angeles, California, Seattle, Boston, and Minnesota. In 1984 the teams that chose exemption were Boston, Los Angeles, Oakland, Pittsburgh, and Philadelphia.

The number of free agents who were classified as A or B was not large.

This was because only the top 30 percent of the players were classified, and most of these did not opt for free agency in a given year. In 1983, for example, only seven players eligible to become free agents were rated A, and three rated B.[15] There were four A-rated players in 1984. Selections from the compensation pool were not particularly controversial. In 1984, however, a free agent transfer upset followers of the New York Mets. The Chicago White Sox lost pitcher Dennis Lamp, who signed as an A-rated player with the Toronto Blue Jays. The White Sox selected Mets pitcher Tom Seaver as compensation for Lamp from among the players in the pool left unprotected by the Mets. Seaver, a valuable player, was lost by the Mets even though they were not a direct participant in the transaction to sign Lamp. This transaction pointed up imperfections in the operation of the compensation system for free agents. Classification of players, despite the use of numerous statistical indicators, is somewhat arbitrary, and clubs may not make the correct choices in protecting players from the compensation pool. The Blue Jays, who signed Lamp, did not lose a player. The free agency market was a kind of Russian Roulette for teams that participated.

The 1982 free agency rules were complex and, in some cases, inequitable. They had little effect in restraining player movement. Perhaps most important, the owners continued to face rapidly escalating salaries. Therefore, in 1985 the rules for free agency were again changed at the bargaining table. Compensation for teams that lose free agents was eliminated. The re-entry draft, in existence since free agency began in 1976, was abolished. Thus, under the new rules, any team is able to sign a free agent without having to select negotiating rights; however, if a free agent's former team wants to retain negotiating rights to him, it must agree to go to salary arbitration with him if he chooses.

The thrust of the new rules is that they lift virtually all impediments to a player's becoming a free agent except the need to fulfill the terms of an existing contract. When that contract expires, the player is free to test the market with other clubs interested in signing him, without the constraint that compensation to his old club entailed. Wide open free agency in baseball has caused a rapid increase in the number of "lifetime" contracts for outstanding players. These contracts will keep these players with their clubs for the remainder of their careers, unless the club decides to trade them.

Free agent signings have had a mixed impact. Some free agents have performed well for their new teams; others have not. From 1982 to 1985, nearly two-thirds of the free agents had significant declines in performance in the first year with their new teams. Although much concern has been expressed over altering the competitive balance of the game, with rich teams in large cities being able to buy up all the good players, teams that have been active in the free agency market have not usually dominated their divisions. The World Series winners from 1982 to 1985 had only two significant free agents: Darrell Porter of St. Louis and Darrell Evans of Detroit. Some teams that have been relatively inactive in signing free agents and depended instead on well-managed farm systems and astute trading have had good success. From its initiation in 1976 through 1979, free agency seemed to have a dampening effect on trading. In 1980 trading began to increase somewhat, but remained at lower levels than in the years before free agency. The level of trading has also been limited by the fact that most top quality players have long-term, guaranteed contracts with "no-trade" clauses that require a player's consent to be traded.

The players have been the chief beneficiaries from free agency. As indicated in table 2.3, salaries started to boom after 1976, when the opportunity for free agency affected a large number of players. They have used their new bargaining muscle to help increase salaries by more than sixfold since then. Individual players have also been able to force other changes in how the game is run. Multiyear contracts, providing greater financial and job security, have become commonplace.[16] Players also have gained more control over their financial destinies by winning contract clauses stating that they can be traded only to certain teams in large cities and thus providing for fatter future contracts. There is also some evidence that free agency has provided higher incomes to black and Hispanic players and reduced salary discrimination based on race.[17]

The record attendance levels for major league baseball in recent years indicate that spectator interest has not waned as a result of free agency—indeed, it has probably been stimulated. Fans do have loyalty to players, but what fans really want is winning players with whom they find immediate allegiance. There is a long tradition in baseball of outstanding players moving from team to team. In the past this occurred as a result of trades, while today's player movement is often the result of free agency. One study found that outstanding players are actually more stable under free agency than they were under the old system.[18] Owners grouse that higher salaries are threatening their solvency, yet it is unlikely that teams pay more than about a third of their revenues in player salaries and pensions, a proportion that has remained relatively constant in spite of free agency.

Salary Arbitration

In the 1973 collective bargaining agreement a key provision affecting player salaries was introduced—salary arbitration. Salary arbitration was first used for the 1974 season and has been continued in subsequent agreements. Under this arrangement, if the team owner and player do not reach agreement on salary, the dispute is submitted to an impartial arbitrator for final decision. Although salary arbitration is also used in professional hockey, a distinguishing feature of baseball arbitration is that the arbitrator is required to choose either the player's demand or the ballclub's offer, with no compromise between the two positions. For example, if the player asks for $400,000 and the team owner offers $300,000, the arbitrator must choose one figure or the other, not something in between.

To be eligible for salary arbitration, the player must have a total of three years of major league experience (until 1987, only two years experience is required). Submission to arbitration is made between January 15 and 25, and hearings are held from February 1 to 20, with one day of hearing scheduled for each case. Each party is limited to one hour for initial presentation and a half hour for rebuttal and summation. Arbitration decisions are due within twenty-four hours of the close of hearing. Instead of the customary written opinion, arbitrators are allowed only to write in the salary figure they choose on the duplicate copies of the Uniform Player's Contract provided them and mail the copies to the appropriate league office. Arbitration provides only one-year contracts.

The criteria for the arbitrator's decision are (1) the player's contribution during the past season, including overall performance, special qualities of leadership, and public appeal, (2) length and consistency of career contribution, (3) past compensation, (4) comparative baseball salaries, (5) existence of any physical or mental defects, and (6) recent performance of the club.

The arbitration clause provides that the arbitrator shall not consider the financial position of the player or club, press comments or testimonials, offers made before arbitration, costs of representation, or salaries in other sports or occupations. The player and club divide equally the cost of the arbitration hearing.

Arbitration decisions in baseball are summarized in table 2.7. No cases were decided in 1976, because negotiations for a new contract were not concluded until after the season began, nor in 1977, because all the players whose contracts expired before the season began were eligible for free agency. The table shows that the owners have won more cases than the players over the years (124–101).

Since 1979, however, the outcomes are nearly even. One reason for the shift is that some team owners have apparently made purposely low offers. While this all but assures that the owners will lose in arbitration, their rationale for this tactic is that while it may cost them more money for a particular player, they may avoid setting a precedent for other players. For instance, if Player B is awarded his offer by the arbitrator, Players C and D who got less in negotiations with the team owner may "blame" the arbitrator more than the owner. On the other hand, this strategy is difficult to sustain

Table 2.7   Arbitration in Major League Baseball, 1974–86

Year	Arbitration Awards	For the Player	For the Club
1974	29	13	16
1975	16	6	10
1978*	9	2	7
1979	14	8	6
1980	26	15	11
1981	21	11	10
1982	22	8	14
1983	30	13	17
1984	10	4	6
1985	13	6	7
1986	35	15	20
Total	225	101	124

Source: Data for 1974–83 from Major League Baseball Player Relations Committee; 1984 data from *Sporting News*, 12 March 1984, 35; 1985 data from *Sporting News*, 11 March 1985, 44; and 1986 data from San Francisco Chronicle, 24 February 1986, 66.

Note: *No cases were heard in 1976 and 1977.

because in following years Players C and D may prefer to go to arbitration rather than settling with the owner in negotiations.

An interesting area for inquiry is the effect that the arbitration process has on negotiations. In theory, the final-offer feature is designed to stimulate negotiations. Under the conventional method of arbitration in wage determination cases, the arbitrator is empowered to compromise between the positions of the parties. That is, if the union wants a 10 percent increase and the employer offers 6 percent, the arbitrator can choose something in between the two positions, say 7 or 8 percent. This method can reduce the parties' incentive to compromise in negotiations because they anticipate that the arbitrator may wind up splitting the difference. Thus, the more realistic of the parties may wind up losing to the side that budged the least. This is known as the chilling effect, since the possibility of compromise by the arbitrator between the positions of the parties reduces their desire to move toward accommodation.

In contrast, final-offer arbitration would seem to encourage the parties to compromise in negotiations because the arbitrator is confined to selecting one or the other position. If either side gets too far out of line, the other's position will be adopted by the arbitrator. Because of an incentive to be as realistic as possible, i.e., wanting to win in arbitration, the parties may reach a common ground through negotiation and eliminate the need for arbitration altogether.

Evidence from the experience with final-offer arbitration in public employment labor disputes tends to support the theory that it reduces the chilling effect and thus preserves negotiation.[19] What does the experience in baseball indicate? A study by James Dworkin found that, considering the large number of salaries that are negotiated between players and clubs each year, the number of arbitration decisions is comparatively small,[20] so that if there is a chilling effect in baseball arbitration, it is minor. A substantial number of eligible players have filed for arbitration, but in recent years a high proportion of these cases have been settled before the arbitration award. For example, in 1981, 74 out of 96 cases were settled; in 1982, 80 out of 103; and in 1985, 85 out of 98.[21]

Salary arbitration has increased player bargaining power by giving them an alternative in situations in which they would otherwise have to settle for what the team is willing to pay them. Free agency's upward pull on salaries has caused the awards in arbitration to rise; higher arbitration settlements, in turn, reflect on what free agents are able to command in the market. The spiraling effects of free agency and salary arbitration account for most of the escalation of player salaries in recent years.

Substance Abuse

Alcoholism has long been a major problem in society and at the workplace. Widespread drug problems are of more recent origin. "Drug abuse," as that term is ordinarily used, refers to the nonmedical consumption of psychoactive substances, such as amphetamines, barbiturates, cocaine, marijuana, LSD, and heroin. The most common effect of drug and alcohol abuse on the job is increased absenteeism; other effects are decline in productivity, decreased motivation to do a good job, and increased employee accidents.[22] Drug abuse has been increasingly recognized as a serious problem affecting workers, and numerous programs for rehabilitation exist in American industry. Testing for drug usage is found in the Armed Forces. In boxing and in Olympic competition, urinalysis is commonly used to test for drugs.

Alcoholism has always existed as a problem for baseball players and for other professional athletes. Healthy, strong, and in the bloom of youth, many athletes drink to relax from the tensions of the games or for bonhomie with their teammates. Between games and during the off-season, players have long periods of free time. Alcohol abuse is not viewed with as much social disapprobation as drug abuse. It is for this reason that baseball players such as Darrell Porter of the St. Louis Cardinals, Bob Welch of the Los Angeles Dodgers, and Dennis Martinez of the Baltimore Orioles, who acknowledged their alcoholism problems and undertook rehabilitation, have received sympathy and even respect from the public.

Drug abuse presents more complex issues because of the diversity of psychoactive substances and the reasons for which they are used. Amphetamines are commonly found in sports locker rooms. When used for getting up for a game, they spark no great protest from the public or club owners. But if used outside the game for social recreation, amphetamines prompt a different response. The public makes similar distinctions between softer drugs such as marijuana and harder ones like cocaine.

Americans are socialized to rely on the quick fix of drugs. They are exposed to a barrage of television commercials advertising drugs to get rid of headaches, relax, stimulate the bowels, and get to sleep. The message is that life and work are difficult, but drugs can help us get by. Players' careers are short and risky. They experience intense pressure to perform at high levels and win. Some players use drugs to help their performance, to make them feel good, or simply to go along with the crowd.

Violations and Penalties

Before 1983 there were some isolated incidents involving drugs in base-ball.[23] Ferguson Jenkins of the Texas Rangers was suspended indefinitely by Commissioner Kuhn in 1980 when cocaine, hashish, and marijuana were found in his luggage at the Toronto airport. He appealed the suspension through the MLBPA, and after a grievance hearing arbitrator Raymond Goetz ordered the suspension lifted with back pay after two weeks. Jenkins eventually was given an "absolute discharge" by a Canadian judge, who found him guilty but did not convict him. His record was cleared when he completed a drug-diversion program and agreed to work with youth groups. In 1982 Allan Wiggins of the San Diego Padres was suspended by his team for one month for possession of cocaine. When Lonnie Smith of the St. Louis Cardinals informed the team that he had a cocaine problem, he underwent treatment without discipline and returned to duty.

In 1983 two incidents brought the cocaine problem in baseball into sharper focus: arrests of four Kansas City Royals players and the suspension of Steve Howe of the Los Angeles Dodgers. In the Kansas City case, the Federal Bureau of Investigation obtained permission to tap the telephone line of a suspected drug dealer and obtained information that eventually led to the arrest and conviction of four Royals players: Willie Wilson, Willie Aikens, and Jerry Martin (for attempting to possess cocaine), and Vida Blue (for possession of cocaine). After plea bargaining, the players pleaded guilty to reduce charges with misdemeanor status, and they were sentenced to ninety days in a federal penitentiary. In the Los Angeles case, Howe was not charged with a crime involving drugs but had undergone several periods of rehabilitation for cocaine use. The Dodgers fined him $54,000 and suspended him indefinitely.

On December 15, 1983, Commissioner Kuhn suspended Wilson, Aikens, Martin, and Howe for one year each, although the three Royals' suspensions were subject to petition for reinstatement on May 15, 1984. After a year

Howe's suspension was reviewed by the commissioner, at which time it was lifted. The penalties imposed on the players by the commissioner were the toughest for drug violations yet handed out and indicated that future abuse would be dealt with severely.

In response to the publicity of the cocaine busts, the MLBPA and the owners formed a joint committee to develop a program for drug and alcohol education. Called the Drugs Study Committee, it has four representatives from management and two from the union. Ken Moffett wanted to involve the union in policing drug abuse issues by disciplining players, but this view was not accepted by other MLBPA leaders who were on the committee, and Moffett's position led to his dismissal. It is therefore not surprising that the union came to the aid of the suspended players by filing grievances. The union argued that it is the government's responsibility to administer the law, not the commissioner's, and that the Royals' players had already been punished by prison terms. Arbitrator Richard Bloch, ruling on the Wilson and Martin grievances, reached a compromise decision. Bloch acknowledged the disciplinary powers of the commissioner, but pre-empted the commissioner by ruling before he could make further review. The players received some measure of vindication by being allowed to return to their team on May 15, 1984. Willie Aikens was allowed by Commissioner Kuhn to resume play at the same time. Vida Blue was suspended for the 1984 season. He was reinstated at the start of the 1985 season by Commissioner Ueberroth. The union filed a grievance on behalf of Steve Howe, but it was later dropped at Howe's request so that he could concentrate on recovering from his cocaine problem. Another player who was suspended by the commissioner in 1984 for cocaine possession, Pascual Perez of the Atlanta Braves, won immediate reinstatement after a grievance decision by arbitrator Bloch.

Control Program

The problems that came to light in the cases of the Royals players underscore the fact that baseball did not have an effective program for dealing with drug abuse. Rather than being involved with management in a cooperative program to resolve the problems, the MLBPA was on the outside as the defender of accused players. No simple solutions existed, but it appeared that a cooperative effort would be better than having the parties view themselves as antagonists on drug issues. Although a joint committee was formed, it initially bogged down on the issue of testing, which the union contended violated players' civil rights. Nevertheless, the management of several teams began testing for drugs and established extensive drug education programs.

In mid-1984 the joint committee talks finally resulted in agreement on a comprehensive drug control program, but this program was terminated by the owners after eighteen months. The program was patterned after the innovative program in basketball, which was also reached through labor-management agreement. Under the program, *drugs* referred to hard drugs like cocaine, but not marijuana or amphetamines. If a club suspected that a player had a drug problem, it discussed the matter with him. If the player did not acknowledge a problem or agree on a course of treatment, the case was to be submitted to a three-member medical panel jointly selected by the owners and players. The panel would then decide whether the club had a valid reason to suspect a player and how best to deal with it. If a player underwent treatment either after assessment by the medical panel or by coming forth voluntarily, he received full salary during off-season treatment or for the first thirty days of in-season care. After thirty more days of half pay, the player received a rate equal to the minimum $40,000 salary until able to play again. The commissioner was empowered under the program to discipline a player if he was convicted on a drug charge, distributed drugs, or used drugs at the ball park. Disciplinary actions were made subject to grievance by the union. Like the arrangement in basketball, baseball's program was designed to give players an incentive to seek help, but was tough on drug violators who did not come forward. Testing was limited to situations where a player was on probation for drug use.

Nearly all the players ratified the drug control program. The owners initially held back because of the absence of mandatory random drug testing provisions, but later approved the program. It was in effect for the remainder of 1984 and was extended for the 1985 season.

Testing Controversy

Although it appeared that baseball's drug problems were well on the way toward resolution, a new scandal erupted in 1985. At drug hearings in Pittsburgh, a jury in federal district court convicted Curtis Strong, former Philadelphia Phillies clubhouse caterer, of selling cocaine to players. Strong was sentenced to twelve years in prison. While no players were on trial, several of them testified. They revealed widespread incidents of cocaine use involving themselves as well as teammates. A growing number of players had tired of protecting drug users. Some twenty-one players were implicated in drug use, and estimates were that as many as 40 percent of all players had used cocaine in the past.

In view of the Pittsburgh hearings and reports in the media that baseball's drug problem was more serious than commonly realized, Commissioner Ueberroth acted decisively. Rather than taking steps to punish individual players, he boldly announced a mandatory drug testing program for all baseball personnel (major and minor leagues), except for major league players represented by the MLBPA. Ueberroth turned up the pressure by making a direct appeal to major league players for their support of mandatory testing. His timing was questionable because negotiations were then underway for a new collective bargaining agreement. Ueberroth's highly publicized proposal to the players not only disrupted negotiations but antagonized the union. Although many players had already indicated their willingness to submit to testing, Donald Fehr's outrage at the commissioner's actions caused the union to close its ranks and refuse to go along. Ueberroth's media blitz and end-run not only failed, but were probably unlawful under the National Labor Relations Act because he did not go through proper channels and pressured the players on a subject over which the union had authority. This incident points up the commissioner's new power in his redefined position, but also some continuing limitation of his power. It was a rare defeat for Ueberroth and somewhat tarnished his reputation among players and owners. At the same time, however, his proposals were probably in the best interests of the sport, and they appear to have had the general approval of the public.

After the dustup over the commissioner's initiatives, he urged that the owners and players meet to discuss testing, thus acknowledging that the issue should be resolved through negotiations. But he tried to keep the pressure on the union by insisting that the union agree in principle to testing before details of a testing program were worked out in negotiations. He also held out the possibility of seeking to punish players implicated in the Pittsburgh hearings. The union continued to resist testing, arguing that it was a violation of the players' civil liberties.

The pressure was turned up another notch when the owners voted during the 1985 World Series to terminate the existing drug control program. This unanimous vote pointed up the owners' conclusion, drawn from the Pittsburgh hearings, that the program was not working. In light of the continuation of the drug scandal, it is likely that the union came to the same conclusion, although it was not inclined to junk the existing program. In any event, circumstances were impelling the union toward a revised program that would require testing. Ueberroth was determined to eliminate drugs from baseball, and many players joined him in this resolve. The union's reticence was understandable because mandatory testing of all players would break new ground in professional team sports. Also, assuming that the players were willing to go along with testing, the union wanted to play a major role in developing and administering a testing program. The details of such a program would take time to work out in negotiations.

The drug testing issue came to a head in March 1986 when Commissioner Ueberroth took action against twenty-one players who were admitted or suspected drug users. Seven admitted users, including star players Keith Hernandez of the New York Mets and Dave Parker of the Cincinnati Reds, were given the alternative of a one-year suspension or donation of 10 percent of their 1986 salaries to drug-prevention programs, one hundred hours of work in drug-related community service over each of the next two years, and submission to random drug testing for the rest of their careers. A second category of players was given the option of a sixty-day suspension or contributing 5 percent of their salaries and fifty hours of community service, plus career-long testing. Players in a third category need only submit to random testing. Ueberroth's actions appear to have been wise and productive. One of the problems former drug offenders have is relapse because of exposure to active users. Ueberroth's decision exposes players to an environment that involves working with youth toward drug prevention and should serve as a reminder to players of the dangers of relapse.

Alternative Solutions

One of the biggest difficulties in any drug control program is getting people to acknowledge their dependency and come forward for help. The individual clubs have had different policies on encouraging disclosure and have varied in their reactions to treatment and penalizing players. Uniformity is needed so that identification and treatment policies are consistent and can be relied on by players. Too few of the players with problems have sought help from their clubs. None of the four Royals players did so before running afoul of the law. Some players simply do not want help, and some feel that getting caught is something that happens to the other guy.

A punishment mentality has characterized the reactions of much of baseball management to violations by players, and some players that owners merely suspect to have drug problems have been quietly peddled to other clubs. Yet it is difficult to see how punitive actions serve a useful purpose. If existing deterrents, such as risk of arrest or damaging performance and career, do not keep players off drugs, it is questionable whether fines and suspensions will do so either. Threat of punishment may, on the other hand, prevent players from coming forth for treatment.

Public outcry is behind the punitive actions. Sports officials have responded to the adverse publicity over drug abuse by coming down hard on the players. Although drug abuse is a crime, it is also an illness that requires medical treatment. It appears that not enough attention has been given to the medical side and too much to the criminal behavior side, and the argument can be made that unless criminal behavior affects the player's performance or integrity of the game, this side of the problem is the business of the police. But because drug abuse affects the integrity of the game's public image and spectator identification with players as role models, baseball tries to keep its house clean. Its hardliners are for cracking down, not coddling. This may well represent the consensus of the public as well, however unproductive such responses may be to resolving the problems. In its initial drug control program, baseball followed basketball in establishing a moderate approach that emphasized both enlightened attitudes toward treatment and punishment for violators who fail to come forth to seek help. It may be necessary, however, to additionally require testing under these programs to ensure public confidence in the moral integrity of professional team sports.

A New Era?

The establishment of drug controls, the changing of the guard in chief negotiators, and a new commissioner with an expanded role in industrial relations may signal a new era in baseball. The past has been fraught with bitter contests between labor and management. These battles were probably inevitable, given the monopoly control that owners had over players. But the constraints have been broken, the conflicts waged, and the players have won their freedom with its accompanying munificence of rewards. The time appears to be at hand when the weapons of industrial conflict can be put aside and a more rational approach taken to the economic problems confronting baseball, more reasoned methods of resolving these problems in collective bargaining.

Given the limitations of his job description, Bowie Kuhn was a good commissioner for baseball. His replacement, Peter Ueberroth is an even more promising executive who seems to have less allegiance to a strict pro-management line. In general, he welcomes the existence of the players' association and appears to recognize the need to further the interests of the industry through greater cooperation on labor-management issues. As the director of the highly successful Los Angeles Olympics, he demonstrated strong leadership, worked closely with unions, and oversaw the making of a $150 million profit. Although Marvin Miller retains some control, new blood represents the union at the bargaining table in chief negotiator Donald Fehr, who proved his mettle in gaining the players' support for the initial drug control program. Lee MacPhail headed the management bargaining team. He is well liked and demonstrated willingness to accommodate on difficult problems. These signs of change are encouraging and suggest that the years of acrimony may be over. Numerous challenges remain, but their resolution should be easier now that a greater equalization of power between labor and management has occurred and new faces are on the scene for problem solving. Two events in this new era suggest a more cooperative future: the umpires' strike and its thoughtful resolution by Ueberroth and the 1984–85 negotiations, which despite a brief strike, led to a replacement agreement that contains provisions meeting the needs of both owners and players.

Umpires' Strike

Officials in professional team sports are well organized into associations that negotiate with management over a variety of work-related issues. Only in football have officials maintained a relatively quiescent role in dealings with the leagues that employ them. Basketball referees have gone on strike, and baseball umpires struck in 1970 and 1979. In each of the umpires' strikes play was disrupted, and after the settlements a residue of bitterness remained, especially against fellow umpires (mostly from the minor leagues) who acted as scabs by crossing picket lines to officiate games. For several years the sixty-man Major League Umpires Association has been represented by a Philadelphia lawyer named Richie Phillips. In the 1984 negotiations with the association, the management bargainers were league presidents Charles Feeney (National League) and Bobby Brown (American League), and at issue was the amount of postseason pay for umpires and how it would be distributed. At the time, umpires received $10,000 for the playoff games and $15,000 for World Series games for a total cost to the leagues of $210,000. Only umpires who worked these events were paid. The umpires asked not only for a sizable increase in pay but also that the monies go into a pool that would be in part distributed to umpires who did not officiate postseason games. They argued that favoritism influenced the merit system selection of umpires for postseason play and that a pool system would provide a more equitable arrangement.

At the outset of the playoffs, just after Ueberroth became commissioner, the umpires went on strike. Bowie Kuhn had forsworn involvement in negotiations when he was commissioner, and Ueberroth initially indicated his intention to do the same. The job description of the commissioner was changed, however, when Ueberroth took office and allowed him to take a more active role in labor relations. Moreover, pressure began to build as playoff games were officiated by minor league umpires. When Phillips asked Ueberroth to intercede in the strike, he was initially reluctant to encroach on the authority of Feeney and Brown who had greater familiarity with the issues in dispute. Later, when all the negotiators agreed to request Ueberroth to arbitrate the impasse, he acted quickly to bring the parties together for a hearing. This arbitration resolved the issues and the umpires returned to work for the fifth and final game of the National League playoffs (the American League playoffs lasted just three games, all of which were umpired by minor league officials).

In his arbitration decision, Ueberroth gave the umpires only slightly less than what they wanted. The pay for umpires went from the previously established $210,000 to $405,000 for 1984, $465,000 for 1985, and $525,000 for 1986. A pool was created for sharing revenues among umpires not working postseason games. Despite what appears to be a one-sided decision in favor of the umpires, Ueberroth was lauded by nearly all observers from both sides, who regarded his ability to resolve the dispute as evidence of strong leadership. One critic was Donald Fehr, director of the players' association, who questioned the commissioner's neutrality in a labor dispute. Fehr was probably apprehensive about the commissioner's role in the forthcoming owner-player negotiations. In any event, it is clear that Ueberroth intends to be a commissioner for all of baseball—not just the owners—and that he will pursue a forceful and active role as its chief executive.

Another strike was threatened by umpires in 1985 over the issue of extra pay for the expanded best-of-seven playoffs. The strike was averted when the parties chose former president Richard M. Nixon, a longtime baseball fan, to arbitrate the dispute. Nixon's decision, his first as an arbitrator, granted a 40 percent salary increase to umpires, which was the same as the percentage increase in the number of games in the league championship series.

1985 Negotiations

The Basic Agreement between the leagues and players' association expired December 31, 1984. Negotiations began in mid-November with hopes that a new contract could be reached before spring training in April 1985. The predominant issue in the talks was distribution of the six-year $1.125 billion television package that began in 1984. Approximately one-third of the monies under the previous television contract had gone into the players' pension fund. In 1983, for example, the contribution amounted to $15.5 million.[24] Under the new television contract, annual revenues increased fourfold, so that if the one-third practice were continued the contribution to the pension fund would rise to about $60 million a year. The owners believed that the pension fund was already quite generous, and they were counting on retaining a larger proportion of the television monies to ensure profitability of club operations.

While the distribution of television revenues was by far the number-one issue, several other points of contention arose. One was the free agency compensation rule, which caused the 1981 strike. The union was dissatisfied with the operation of this rule, despite substantial amounts received by some free agents, and the owners wanted to increase the compensation required for teams that lose free agents. The union vowed to fight any retrenchment in players' free agency rights. Another issue was salary arbitration, which the union wanted to change to allow players to use the procedure after one year of service instead of the existing eligibility of two years.

The owners wanted to increase the eligibility requirement for salary arbitration to three years. The union sought an increase in minimum salaries. An issue pushed by the owners was expansion of the maximum number of playoff games from five to seven games (the same number as the World Series), which the union countered with demands for a share of revenues resulting from the expanded number of games.

The high hopes for an early settlement were dashed by several events that intruded on negotiations. First, the parties delayed getting their demands on the table, a problem that has plagued baseball and other sports in the past. The parties played a cat-and-mouse game of waiting for the other side to make its move. Another problem was that shortly after negotiations began, Houston Astros owner John McMullen commented publicly that union leaders had too much control over the players. This is the kind of ill-considered remark, characteristic of some sports owners, that accomplishes nothing except to antagonize the union. The baseball owners later had to collectively recant by stating that McMullen's views did not reflect those of management in general. Then there was the flap over an attempt by the Los Angeles Dodgers to provide for mandatory drug testing in the contracts of some of its players. Although this dispute blew over quickly when the union forced withdrawal of the provision from the player contracts, it caused another delay in negotiations.

A more troublesome interruption occurred in February when the owners requested a moratorium on talks in order to review a "serious financial situation." This was a familiar story, with the owners pleading poverty in response to union demands. Despite requests by the union in the past, the owners had persistently refused to open their books. Although the legality of such refusals had not been fully tested for baseball, it is well known from NLRB precedent that the National Labor Relations Act requires management to show proof of financial problems if it claims inability to pay. Supposedly, twenty-two of the twenty-six teams in the major leagues were losing money, but which teams and how much was unknown to the union. Probably in recognition of the need for compliance with the law, Commissioner Ueberroth urged the owners to open their books to the MLBPA. When the owners provided team financial data to the union, a dispute arose over interpretation of the data. Both the owners and the union hired outside consultants to review the data. The reports of the consultants—Roger Noll, a Stanford University economics professor acting for the union, and George

Sorter, a New York University accounting professor acting for the owners—were inconclusive. Sorter found the losses to be $27 million rather than the $43 million originally claimed by the owners.[25] Noll did not provide an overall assessment, but found with few exceptions that the teams were profitable, averaging $1 to 2 million per team.[26] It did appear, however, that the financial problems of the owners were likely to worsen in the future unless some kind of limit was placed on expenditures. This limit was proposed by the owners in the form of a salary cap, which would limit high-paying clubs from signing free agents. But this proposal was later dropped by the owners when Commissioner Ueberroth indicated his opposition to the idea.

Players' Strike

As negotiations dragged on with limited progress, the players voted against striking the all-star game in July, but overwhelmingly supported the MLBPA executive board's recommendation to strike on August 6, 1985. There was speculation that Ueberroth might force the owners into a settlement by invoking a clause in baseball's charter to act in the "best interests of the game." The commissioner, however, prudently stayed on the sidelines while encouraging the parties to work hard to achieve a settlement. As the strike deadline approached, negotiations intensified. These discussions centered on two issues: the owners' contribution to the players' benefit plan, which covers pensions and health insurance, and the length of time required for salary arbitration eligibility.

Although no one really wanted a strike, the players walked out on August 6. The parties, however, had been close to agreement at the time, and after just two days, the strike was settled with little cost to the public image of the sport. Most of the games lost were made up later, and the strike had no significant impact on the continuity of the season.

In the end, both sides gave in to get a five-year compromise agreement that was to expire in 1989. The players gained mostly from the increased contribution of monies to their benefit plan, with the owners agreeing to contribute $196 million over six years. While the players' share of national television revenue dropped from the previous 33 percent to 18 percent, they more than doubled the dollar contributions. A ten-year player would receive a pension of about $90,000 annually at age sixty-two. On the other hand, the owners prevailed on their key salary arbitration demand, so that players will have to wait three years instead of the previously required two years before being able to arbitrate their salaries. Minimum salaries were increased from $40,000 to $60,000, with cost-of-living increases for future years.

Another important feature of the agreement was that a $20 million fund was established from network television revenues to aid disadvantaged clubs in smaller cities that were losing the most money. Graduated payments are now made to the players' benefit plan, as clubs no longer contribute equally. The amounts paid by clubs are based on attendance and television market size. This feature may open the door to greater revenue sharing among teams, but it is apt to become a source of controversy as the wealthy teams seek to maintain their prerogatives.

At the very least, Commissioner Ueberroth was instrumental in acting as a catalyst to settling the strike quickly, by prodding the negotiators to keep talking. Perhaps the real hero was Lee MacPhail, whose calm and kindly persuasiveness helped placate the owners he represented. Although it is unfortunate that the strike occurred, all the principals deserve credit for keeping the negotiations in a gentlemanly mode and avoiding the stridency and acrimony that have characterized baseball negotiations in the past. In this sense, baseball seems to be entering a new era in which disagreements can be worked out through cooperation.

3. Football

Professional football has lagged behind baseball in equalizing the imbalance of power between owners and players through collective bargaining. Despite the presence of rival leagues that have raised football salaries, the players' union has lacked the strong, imaginative leadership found in baseball, although it has gained ground toward reducing the control of the owners and commissioner over the game and distribution of its revenues. Much of the intersport disparity lies in the economics of the game. Although the sport is ideally suited for television viewing and the teams receive large revenues from television contracts, the number of players on a football team far exceeds those in other sports. Number of games played is also considerably fewer. These factors limit both labor market opportunities for players and the product market for owners.

The game of football was derived from rugby, which began around 1840 in England. Football started in the United States in the 1870s with games between colleges. In 1876 the Intercollegiate Football Association was organized. Although the game played was essentially the same as rugby, over the years the association's rules changed the game into the football we know today. In 1920 the first major professional football league was formed, with famous college player Jim Thorpe as president.[1] Known as the American Professional Football Association, its teams were poorly managed, and salaries were minimal. The twelve-team league folded after a year, but was reorganized in 1921. The following year its name was changed to the National Football League (NFL). Little success was achieved by the NFL in attracting public attention until the Chicago Bears signed Harold ("Red") Grange in 1925. Grange, a star halfback at the University of Illinois, was known as the Galloping Ghost, and his play with the Bears brought large crowds to watch professional football for the first time.

Gradually the NFL became well established. Early rival leagues were unable to keep going for long. They were the American Football League, which lasted only one year in 1926; another American Football League (1936–37); and the All-America Football Conference (1946–49). When the All-America Football Conference folded, three of its teams—Cleveland, Baltimore, and Los Angeles—became a part of the NFL. The NFL began drafting college players in 1936, which helped provide a steady stream of quality talent. Following Elmer Layden as NFL commissioner (1941–46), Bert Bell provided strong leadership from 1946 to 1959 that helped the league to prosper. It was not until the 1960s, however, that the professional game began to reach big-time status as a result of widespread television exposure.

Economics of Football

The economics of football are influenced by two principal factors: sources of revenue and costs of operation.[2] The determinants of revenues include the number of teams and games played; the size of stadiums and parking and concession arrangements; marketability to broadcast media; tax laws; ticket prices and ticket sales. Cost determinants primarily involve compensation to players, scouts, and front office staff; arrangements for stadium rentals; and equipment, travel, and publicity expenses. Unlike baseball, football does not sustain the cost of maintaining a farm system of minor league teams, since nearly all professional football players are recruited from colleges.

Compared with other major team sports, however, football has certain disadvantages. With forty-five players per team, rosters are far larger than for other sports. There are about fifteen hundred players in the NFL, compared with about six hundred in baseball's major leagues. With sixteen regular season games, plus four preseason games and playoffs, football has a significantly smaller number of playing dates.

On the other hand, football revenues are enhanced considerably by large stadiums that are usually sold out, at least among NFL teams. The cost of the average ticket has risen steadily from about $10.50 in 1981 to $15.00 in 1982 to an estimated $17.00 in 1984. Gate receipts are divided, with 60 percent going to the home team and 40 percent to the visiting team for regular season NFL games and 50 percent each for preseason games.

Television Revenues

Most important to football's economic viability is its unique adaptability to television. Popularity of the sport is unprecedented. Although some declines began to appear in television ratings for NFL games in 1983 and 1984, largely as a result of oversaturation of football from the United States Football League (USFL); ratings began to increase again in 1985. Viewing the games on the television has become an American institution, and millions of viewers are glued to their sets on Sundays and on Monday nights. The money paid by advertisers for commercials on these games is a cornucopia for the television networks, who have provided the NFL with bountiful contracts for broadcast rights.

Under the NFL contracts with CBS, NBC, and ABC that expired in 1981, each of the twenty-eight teams in the league received about $5.8 million. In 1982 a new five-year agreement was reached in which the networks pay the teams an average of $14.2 million a season. These television contracts may seem a glorious example of the success of free enterprise in a capitalistic economy, yet, ironically, they point up the economic influence of the NFL as a cartel and its sharing of television monies equally among teams. Unlike baseball, basketball, and hockey, which show games on local free television or on a pay cable basis, the NFL game is presented entirely through the national television agreements.

An interesting question for the future is whether the NFL will renew its contracts with the networks when they expire in 1987. Pay television is gaining momentum and may by that time present an attractive alternative to the NFL. The USFL already receives a sizable portion of its television revenues from cable, as do the National Basketball Association and the National

Hockey League. Currently, the NFL has an exemption from antitrust law insofar as pooling of broadcast income is concerned. Should the NFL decide to remove games from free public television by contracting with pay television companies, it is possible that Congress would revoke the income pooling exemption. This would cause competition among teams for television revenues and diminish the hegemony of the league.

Tax Advantages

As in other professional sports, an important factor in maintaining the structure and economic success of professional football is that franchises allow for lucrative tax arrangements. Before the Tax Reform Act of 1976, owners were allowed to depreciate 95 percent of the cost of the players over five years. This allowed owners, many of whom were involved in other business enterprises, to show a loss on the team operation while pocketing large sums from ownership of the sports franchise.

Under current rules, owners purchasing a team can allocate only 50 percent of the cost of the franchise to player costs, to be depreciated over five years. This still presents rewarding financial opportunities, however. Suppose, for example, that a football team is purchased for $50 million. Half that amount can be depreciated over five years as a $5 million deduction each year. Owners who make money on team operations pay little or no taxes, and those who lose money on paper can still turn a handsome profit.

When liberalized depreciation is linked with substantial television and gate revenues, team ownership virtually guarantees a profit. Long-term profitability is illustrated by the fact that in 1960 the Dallas Cowboys were purchased by Clint Murchison for $600,000 and sold in 1984 to an eleven-person consortium for $75 million. Also in 1984, the Denver Broncos, which had been purchased for about $33.5 million in 1981, were sold for $70 million. In 1985, the Philadelphia Eagles were sold for $65 million, and the New Orleans Saints for $64 million.

There is not much incentive for teams to win or improve. Consider the case of the Los Angeles Rams, which probably has the highest gross income and costs of operation in the NFL. The Rams' stadium in Anaheim has a capacity of nearly 70,000. For 1983, income from ticket sales and luxury boxes is estimated conservatively at approximately $11 million. Adding in television payments would raise the income figure to about $23 million.

Table 3.1   Los Angeles Rams' Expenditures, 1983

Player salaries	$ 5,000,000
Training camp	400,000
Off-season camp	30,000
Mini camp	35,000
Off-season training	175,000
Trainers	100,000
Equipment	200,000
Operating expenses*	6,000,000
Coaching expenses	3,000,000
Other payments to players	3,000,000
Total	$17,940,000

Source: Author's estimates based primarily on data reported in *Los Angeles Times*, 24 March 1982, part 3, 1; and 3 March 1983, part 3, 2.

Note: *Includes travel expenses and salaries for nonplayer personnel.

Although teams rarely disclose cost data, expenditures for the Rams in 1981 were made available to the NFLPA. These data, as well as other published information for updating estimates to 1983, are shown in table 3.1. The estimate of total operating expenses is about $18 million. Thus, despite a record of winning less than half their games from 1981 to 1983, the Rams made a sizable profit in 1983.

Structure of Employment

NFL and Rival Leagues

During the 1960s, under the direction of the new commissioner, Alvin ("Pete") Rozelle, who was formerly general manager of the Los Angeles Rams, NFL attendance soared to 90 percent of stadium capacities, and millions of persons found a new way to spend their Sundays, watching the games on television. The 1960s were not entirely placid for the NFL, however. In 1963 Commissioner Rozelle suspended Paul Hornung of the Green

Bay Packers and Alex Karras of the Detroit Lions for betting on league games and associating with gamblers. Five other players were fined for betting. The suspension of Hornung and Karras was lifted after eleven months. Another, more important, problem for the NFL was the formation of a rival league.

The NFL's domination was challenged in 1960 when the American Football League (AFL) began play. It was formed the year before by Texas oilman Lamar Hunt, who became its first president. Cities with the first AFL franchises were Buffalo, Boston, Houston, Dallas, Los Angeles, Oakland, Denver, and New York. Although a measure of credibility and financial support for the fledgling league was provided when a major television network, ABC, agreed to televise selected games, the AFL had to struggle for public recognition in the early years. Clubs had few big-name players and inadequate television coverage. The league nearly folded when the New York Titans fell heavily into debt and approached bankruptcy. Although located in the nation's biggest product market, the Titans had few followers and were poorly managed. Coming to the rescue was a five-member syndicate headed by entertainment agent David ("Sonny") Werblin. They purchased the sinking Titans in 1963, hired Weeb Ewbank, a successful coach for the Baltimore Colts in the NFL, and changed the name of the team to the New York Jets.

The turning point for the AFL came in 1964, when Werblin negotiated a five-year television contract with CBS for $36 million, with each team guaranteed $900,000 per year. This additional income allowed the AFL to bid for talented players with the NFL. Werblin and Oakland Raiders' owner Al Davis, who later became president of the AFL, touted the star system idea, a strategy in which the new league would try to sign exceptional players out of college, especially quarterbacks. In a bidding war with the NFL, Werblin signed quarterback Joe Namath from the University of Alabama for an unprecedented $427,000 over four years. Other young stars out of college signed large contracts: John Hadl from the University of Kansas, Lance Alworth from San Diego State, Fred Biletnikoff from Florida State, and Mike Garrett, winner of the Heisman trophy at the University of Southern California. The AFL was clearly in business as a formidable rival to the NFL and was costing teams in the older league millions of dollars in competition for players.

To end escalating competition, the NFL and AFL agreed to merge in 1966, thus establishing a common draft of players. AFL clubs agreed to pay NFL clubs a total of $18 million in principal and interest over the next twenty years. The leagues played separate schedules until 1970, when their television contracts expired. In 1967 the first Super Bowl game was played between the NFL and AFL champions. The merged league originally consisted of twenty-six teams (by 1976 the number had grown to the current twenty-eight teams with the addition of NFL franchises in Seattle and Tampa Bay). Pete Rozelle remained commissioner of the unified league.

In 1974 another rival league began direct competition with the NFL. The World Football League (WFL) was created by Gary Davidson, who earlier had established competitive leagues in professional basketball and hockey. NFL players welcomed the twelve-team operation because it would give them opportunities to jump to a new league for higher salaries and cause upward pressure on all football salaries. The WFL gained some credibility when its Toronto franchise signed three players from the NFL's Miami Dolphins. These players—Larry Csonka, Paul Warfield, and Jim Kiick—received contracts with a total value of about $3 million.

In 1975, however, the WFL folded in the middle of its second season of play, leaving about 380 players without jobs. Some of these players were acquired by NFL teams. Several factors contributed to the demise of the WFL. Although most of its franchises were located in non-NFL cities, attendance was poor. Few big-name players signed with the league, which worked against its efforts to establish public visibility. Without adequate television exposure, ownership lacked financial resiliency, and franchises shifted to other cities or went bankrupt. Perhaps most important, the rival league played its games at the same time as the NFL and was viewed by the public as an inferior alternative.

A new and more formidable rival to the NFL, the United States Football League (USFL), began play in 1983 with twelve teams, each playing a twenty-game season from March through June and a championship game in early July. Realizing the importance of television, the USFL chose as its commissioner Chet Simmons, former president of NBC Sports and chief executive officer of ESPN, a sports cable television network.

The USFL avoided at least three of the problems that plagued the WFL. First, it was not in direct competition with the NFL because games were played in the spring and early summer rather than the traditional fall season. Second, the USFL had owners that possessed strong financial staying power since they were among the richest people in America. Third, the USFL lined up a two-year television contract with ABC and another contract with ESPN. These contracts, negotiated before the USFL began play, provided greater national television exposure than the WFL had. Also, the USFL was in larger cities than the WFL and had more high-quality stadiums in which to play.

Although the USFL was mostly stocked with players who were marginal in the NFL, the new league utilized the philosophy of the old AFL by creating a star system. By holding its draft of college players before the NFL's, the USFL was able to sign some of the finest college talent in its first year of operation: Kelvin Bryant from North Carolina, Anthony Carter from Michigan, Trumaine Johnson from Grambling, and 1983 Heisman trophy winner Herschel Walker from Georgia. The deep pockets of USFL owners, such as Donald Trump of the New Jersey Generals and J. William Oldenburg of the Los Angeles Express, were evident in the tremendous salaries offered to lure top college players and NFL veterans to their teams. In its second year of operation, the USFL expanded to eighteen teams and continued rapidly signing such attractive college players as Heisman trophy winner Mike Rozier from Nebraska and Steve Young from Brigham Young, as well as NFL stars such as Joe Cribbs and Doug Williams. The pace slowed in 1985, but Heisman winner Doug Flutie from Boston College signed with New Jersey.

In the 1985 season, there was a significant restructuring of the USFL. Beset with low television ratings and losses estimated at $80 million in the previous year, the league reduced the number of teams from eighteen to fourteen. It also announced plans to shift from a spring to fall schedule in 1986. These changes may be a death knell for the USFL because they point up the franchises' decreasing ability to operate successfully and place the USFL in direct competition with the NFL. The older league has high-quality play and a dominance of television exposure that will make it difficult for the USFL to retain fans. Because the NFL dominates television on Sundays and Monday nights and the networks are legally barred from presenting professional games on Friday nights or Saturdays during the college football season, the USFL will narrow its scheduling opportunities for presenting games. It will also run into problems with use of stadium facilities, some of which will have to be shared with NFL teams. At the end of the 1985 season, several star players in the USFL signed with NFL teams.

NFLPA

The idea of a union of football players was conceived in 1954 by two Cleveland Browns players, Abe Gibron and Dante Lavelli, who suggested it to Creighton Miller, a former Browns player who was then serving as the team's attorney. Two years later the National Football League Players Association (NFLPA) was formally organized at a meeting before the 1956 NFL championship game. Miller became legal counsel for the new union. The NFLPA initially signed up members from all NFL teams. At first the owners would not deal with the new union. Then a decision by the U.S. Supreme Court in 1957 finding football to be subject to the antitrust laws prompted the union to threaten the owners with a $4.2 million antitrust suit. Using this threat, Miller was able to get the owners to agree to a $5,000 minimum salary, $50 for each exhibition game played, and an injury clause that continued a player's salary and provided medical and hospital care. In 1959 the union achieved another breakthrough when it persuaded the owners to provide a pension plan for the players.

The NFLPA was registered with the U.S. Department of Labor as a labor union in 1968. At this time, the player representatives from the sixteen NFL teams voted unanimously to reject an attempt by the Teamsters Union to organize the players. Creighton Miller resigned and was replaced by Chicago lawyer Daniel S. Schulman, who became the chief negotiator and legal counsel for the union. Despite his resignation as the union's legal counsel, Miller continued to be active in football labor relations as an agent representing players.

Edward R. Garvey became executive director of the NFLPA in 1971. Under his leadership, the union became more aggressive at the bargaining table and in the courtroom. He led the union when it shut down training camps for forty-two days in 1974, and as a lawyer, he was also instrumental in getting the courts to nullify the Rozelle Rule, discussed later. In 1979 the NFLPA became the first professional sports organization to receive a charter as an affiliate of the AFL-CIO, and Garvey was chosen to be the head of a new organization within the AFL-CIO, called the Federation of Professional Athletes, an umbrella group for the welfare of sports unions.

Garvey represented the union in other skirmishes with the NFL and its commissioner, acting to enhance the union's ability to bargain over certain issues and to check the power of the commissioner over players. Throughout collective bargaining during Garvey's tenure, the NFL owners refused to negotiate over numerous issues the players felt affected their working conditions. In one case, the National Labor Relations Board determined that the issue of artificial turf on playing fields was a mandatory subject for bargaining. The union had argued that artificial turf is a working condition in that players sustain a higher number of injuries on this kind of playing surface. Although the NLRB found the issue to be one that must be negotiated, it did not find that management had failed to bargain in good faith on this issue.[3] The upshot of this ruling was that while the union has the right to bargain over artificial turf, management's obligation is to negotiate sincerely on the subject in good faith, not necessarily to agree to change its policy. A later NLRB decision reinforced the union's right to negotiate over football rules that involve player safety.[4]

Another decision by the NLRB determined that the commissioner has power to enact a rule prohibiting players from leaving the bench area during fights and automatically fining those players who do. This decision, however, was appealed to the courts, which overturned the NLRB decision and found the NFL guilty of an unfair labor practice.[5] This decision further underscores the general rule that management has to negotiate with the union on matters affecting their wages, hours, or working conditions. Unilateral actions by management, without consultation with the union, will not be allowed if they encroach on the subjects over which the union has rights of representation.

An important function performed by unions is enforcement of the collective bargaining agreement through the grievance procedure. A union tries to settle disputes over the interpretation or application of the contract with management in a process in which unresolved grievances move upward through the steps of the procedure to higher levels of labor and management authority. In nearly all grievance procedures negotiated by unions, the final step is arbitration by an outside neutral. In baseball negotiations, the union was successful in winning the right to arbitrate and then using the arbitration step of the grievance procedure to preserve and even expand its status as a player representative.

The NFLPA has limited rights to arbitrate grievances, which have been established in its collective bargaining agreements through the years. Before these changes, the commissioner had the final say on all grievances. Even today, authority for certain areas of contract interpretation and discipline, which are usually under the purview of arbitration clauses in other sectors of private industry, remains in the hands of the commissioner. A case in point is discipline for drug-related violations.

In the 1970 agreement, arbitration was provided for disputes over player injuries. Although Ed Garvey was not executive director of the NFLPA at the time this contract was negotiated, he worked for the law firm that served as legal counsel to the union and thus was involved in negotiations. Under the negotiated agreement, a list of neutral orthopedic physicians was selected by management and the union. Employer defenses to paying injured players included demonstration that the player did not pass his physical examination, that the injury occurred from nonfootball causes, and that the player had not aggravated an old injury. If a dispute arose involving an injury, it was submitted to an impartial arbitrator, who decided whether the player was entitled to compensation under his contract with the team. The provision for arbitration of injury grievances has been continued in later agreements.

In 1977 the scope of arbitration was extended to include noninjury grievances. Although a grievance was defined as "any dispute . . . involving the interpretation or application of, or compliance with, provisions of this Agreement. . . ," various exclusions were made to the definition of a grievance and therefore to the kinds of grievances that could be submitted to arbitration.[6] For instance, the commissioner retained the right to rule on matters affecting the "integrity of or public confidence in" football and disciplinary matters involving players as stated in their standard player contracts. These provisions were continued in the 1982 collective bargaining agreement.

An important new section included in the 1982 agreement involves screening of player agents by the NFLPA. Unlike its practice in past agreements, the union did not waive its right under the National Labor Relations Act to negotiate with teams over individual player salaries:

Other Compensation: A player will be entitled to receive a signing or reporting bonus, additional salary payments, incentive bonuses and such other provisions as may be negotiated between his club (with the assistance of the Management Council) and the NFLPA or its agent. The club and the NFLPA or its agent will negotiate in good faith over such other compensation; provided, however, that a club will not be required to deal with the NFLPA or its agent on a collective or tandem basis for two or more players on that club.[7]

What this provision means is that should the NFLPA choose to do so, it could negotiate individual player salaries. As yet there is no indication that the union is negotiating these salaries. In 1984 the NFLPA had a policy that no staff member may represent a player in individual contract negotiations.[8] It does, however, require agents to get approval from the NFLPA in order to represent players. The reason for this screening is to help ensure that the provisions of the 1982 agreement and the law are complied with and that players receive effective and responsible agent representation in their individual salary negotiations. Another provision of the 1982 agreement required that the NFLPA receive copies of all individual player contracts. This enabled the union to have complete salary data on players for the first time.

Over the years, Ed Garvey survived several attempts by the membership in the NFLPA to oust him as executive director. Controversy over his leadership peaked after the fifty-seven-day strike in 1982. Despite what appeared to be his imminent dismissal by the players, the union's executive committee, composed of player representatives, voted twenty to seven to retain Garvey in office. This committee decision in support of Garvey meant that a vote of the entire union membership was not required. Although he could have stayed on as executive director, the strike and lack of solidarity among the entire membership over his leadership placed a heavy strain on him. Garvey resigned from the union in 1983 to become deputy attorney general in his home state of Wisconsin.

He was replaced as executive director of the NFLPA by Gene Upshaw, who for the previous three years had been president of the NFLPA and was a former star player for the Oakland Raiders. Upshaw has taken a far more moderate tone in dealing with management. As he described the situation, "It's reconstruction, sort of like after the Civil War. . . . We need a change in philosophy . . . I want our image changed."[9] Upshaw's softer line became evident when he took a mild approach on the suspension of players by Commissioner Rozelle for drug abuse. He has also been in close touch with the commissioner and management representatives, indicating that he is trying to build a relationship of trust through more open communication. Grievances that would likely have gone to arbitration in the past have been settled by Upshaw. The union's heavy financial debt has been reduced under his leadership, its costs of operation have declined, and its public image as a particularly fractious organization has changed for the better.

An important challenge facing Upshaw was that of bringing his union together with the players in the USFL. In 1983 the USFL Players Association submitted a petition with the NLRB to represent players in the new league. Two other groups, one headed by agent Michael Trope and another by New York attorney Ron Baron, later joined forces to get on the ballot. In the initial election the USFL players preferred their own organization over the Trope-Baron group by a considerable margin, but because the NLRB challenged several votes and there were numerous votes for no union, a runoff election was held. In the runoff election the players voted 732 to 25 to unionize. Although the USFL Players Association is considered a separate entity, it is joined together with the NFLPA through their mutual affiliation with the Federation of Professional Athletes, AFL-CIO, which Upshaw heads. Achieving an alliance with USFL players enhances the strength of the NFLPA and provides protection for players who move between the two leagues.

Douglas Allen, former assistant director of the NFLPA, became the first executive director of the USFL Players Association. In mid-1984 the union began negotiations with the league. The players sought a high scale for minimum salaries, medical insurance, a pension plan, severance pay, a grievance procedure, and other benefits similar to those achieved by their NFL brethren. The owners' principal demand was a salary cap on team payrolls. Although tentative agreement was reached on several issues, it took almost a year for a contract to be completed. The union's power to strike was virtually nonexistent because a work stoppage would imperil the league's future, and this lack of power limited the union's ability to push negotiations to finality. Because of the problems earlier experienced by the NFLPA and NFL caused by disclosure of bargaining details to the media, the negotiations of the USFL and its union were secluded from publicity except for occasional progress reports.

On March 29, 1985, a four-year agreement was reached between the USFLPA and the league. The principal features of this agreement were (1) a minimum salary of $22,500 for rookies, with graduated increases to $30,000 in 1988; (2) major medical insurance for players and their families of $1 million, plus life and dental insurance; (3) increased preseason per diem to $150 a week for rookies and $200 a week for veterans in 1986, with further increases for later years; (4) increased pay for postseason play, including

$5,000 for members of the losing team in the 1986 championship game, and $10,000 for the winners; and (5) arbitration for both injury and noninjury grievances, but final resolution by the commissioner on disciplinary matters.

Adversary Bargaining

Collective bargaining in football has been characterized by a curious blend of workers who find strikes to be antithetical to their image of professional dedication and an adversary relationship that impels workers to withhold their services if necessary to enhance their economic well-being. Perhaps the closest analogy in other sectors to football players is certain public employees, especially those involved in health and safety services. Police officers, firefighters, and nurses, for example, have a keen sense of psychological attachment to their professions, but also realize the need to seek to maximize their economic reward by opposing the employer with pressure tactics in bargaining.

These incongruent objectives were brought into sharp focus during the fifty-seven-day football strike in 1982. Conflict can cause lack of solidarity among workers if they differ in the values assigned to maintaining public service on the one hand and financial gain on the other. Like public employees, however, professional athletes usually tend to allow their economic objective to overshadow the dedication to job and public if the stakes are high enough. But this does not make the reconciliation of opposing philosophies any less difficult for the participants.

Attitudes

The conflict between financial and professional service goals is particularly acute for football players. The sociocultural environment of their sport promotes obedience and dedication. Football is a team game that does not encourage individuality. Unlike other professional athletes, most football players rarely handle the ball. The running of plays is a highly coordinated effort that emphasizes the interdependence of individuals in the unit and their sacrifice for a common objective.

It is unusual for football players to defy authority. Their environment is paramilitary, well ordered, and authoritarian. It is distinctly two-dimensional, with the coach at the top and the players on the bottom. Youngsters who aspire to careers in the sport are taught the rigid organizational structure and the need for discipline from Pop Warner kid leagues through high school and college. It would be difficult for a player to move through this ritualistic progression without deriving a potent sense of identification with team play and the football establishment.

Players generally view themselves as athletes, not union men, as quite apart from machinists, plumbers, coal miners, and other organized workers. Members of other unions that strike can afford to take a longer view. They have more time to recoup the losses. But football players, who have the shortest career expectancy of any professional athletes, are reluctant to strike because they have more to lose and less time to make it up. They also feel less compunction about breaking a strike by returning to work, since they can be replaced by other players who are willing to work. Only if there is unusual solidarity among all players could they expect to achieve gains by striking.

In addition to the rigid organizational roles that football players are molded into, they are also captives of their own image. Players are lionized by the broadcast and print media and worshiped by a legion of fans; yet they are fearful of the encroachment of age and the fragility of their skills and bodies. Thus the delicate balance of adulation, fear of failure, and team's control over players creates an environment in which it is difficult for players to even contemplate a strike.

Tactics

Despite the players' inherent aversion to strikes, they belong to a union that became increasingly militant under Ed Garvey's leadership. The evolution of the NFLPA into a strident force against management control was a major cause of the 1982 strike. For several years before the strike the union had shown a growing willingness to use pressure tactics to achieve its objectives. Collective bargaining between the NFLPA and NFL is characterized by an adversary relationship, and underlying this relationship is the assumption that the goals of labor and management are in conflict. The NFLPA is seeking to maximize the economic return to players. Management in the NFL is seeking to preserve and protect its revenue sources from interference by the union.

Football

Figure 3.1   Offensive and Defensive Bargaining Tactics

NFLPA	NFL Management
Offensive Tactics	
Strike	Lockout
Picketing	Layoff (cutting dissident players)
Urging direct boycott by fans	Withholding benefits
Urging secondary boycott by firms doing business with owners	Fines
	Influencing public opinion against the union through the media
Influencing public opinion against management through the media	Canceling the season
Form a new league	
Defensive Tactics	
Strike fund	Strike insurance
Financial aid from other unions, e.g., AFL-CIO affiliates	Strike fund
Arranging loans for strikers	Hire strikebreakers
Helping strikers find temporary jobs	Mutual aid, e.g., strike against one club is a strike against all
	Loans to financially ailing clubs
Union-sponsored all-star games	Defending the righteousness of the owners' position to media
Defending the righteousness of the union's position to media	

At bottom, the conflict between the adversaries is over players' salaries: how much they are going to get and how much the owners will have to give up. There are other issues of importance, such as player health and safety, but compensation is predominant. This is similar to bargaining in industries outside sport characterized by adversary bargaining in which the philosophies of union and management negotiators emphasize that division of the wealth of the industry will result from confrontation, or a strike if necessary. The history of the relationship of the adversaries influences their stance. If strikes and other acts of defiance have typified their past dealings, agreement on contract terms may be harder to reach.

The adversary approach in collective bargaining often results in economic loss to both sides. The parties' tactics are calculated either to increase the ability to inflict damage on the opponent (offensive factors), or to enhance one's own ability to withstand pressure from the other side (defensive fac-

70

tors). Figure 3.1 shows offensive and defensive tactics that might be used in football negotiations.

The offensive and defensive factors indicated in figure 3.1 are illustrative, rather than inclusive, of the available tactics. Some of these tactics—such as secondary boycotts, releasing players because of their union activities, and fines—may be challenged in proceedings with the NLRB or the courts as violating federal labor law. Certain of them have been used by the adversaries in football, e.g., strike, lockout, and picketing; others have not been used thus far, e.g., strike insurance, withholding benefits, and union strike fund. The point is that there is an arsenal from which the parties can choose weapons to promote their objectives.

Strike of 1982

NFL players first struck in 1968 over pension fund contributions. Players boycotted training camps, and the owners retaliated with a lockout. After ten days, a compromise agreement was reached, and the job action had no effect on the regular season. Another strike and lockout of training camps, this time for twenty days, occurred in 1970 when pensions, postseason compensation, and a grievance procedure for players were in dispute. These early walkouts were relatively mild forms of protest and were not characterized by much hostility and acrimony between the contestants.

In 1974, however, with a full slate of demands on the bargaining table, the players struck training camps for forty-two days in a bitter dispute. They were particularly upset over freedom issues, including the hated Rozelle Rule, which allowed the commissioner to award compensation for the signing of free agents. This walkout was especially hard on the NFLPA because player solidarity broke down when numerous veteran players crossed picket lines to start training. Most of the disputed issues remained unresolved, and the owners won a clear victory that gave them a heady feeling of power over the union in the 1982 negotiations.

The players' most controversial demand in 1982 was that 55 percent of the gross revenues in the NFL be placed in a fund for distribution to them in salaries and pensions. Adopting a rigid posture, the owners hired Jack Donlan, a tough veteran negotiator, to represent them, and arranged a $150 million line of credit to cushion the impact of a strike. As the fruitless talks

71

continued, the players modified their demand for a fixed percentage to a demand for a wage scale that would base compensation on seniority and be funded out of television revenues. This demand was also met with stiff resistance from the owners. In the face of little progress, the union indicated it would strike between the second and fourth weeks of the regular season, and after completion of the second week of games, the players walked out.

As the strike progressed, the NFL offered $1.6 billion of guaranteed money to the union, in effect accepting a version of revenue sharing. But how the money was to be divided among players and the period to which it would apply remained in dispute. The parties tried mediation, bringing in Sam Kagel, a distinguished neutral from San Francisco. Confronted with the antagonisms of the chief negotiators and the chaotic scene at the bargaining table, there was little that Kagel could do. Successful mediation depends on a willingness of the parties to respond to prodding, which did not exist during Kagel's efforts.

The players showed surprising solidarity for much of the strike. They even staged all-star games and threatened to form a new league. Their efforts at offsetting the financial deprivation of the strike were not successful, however. Dissent in the ranks over continuing the strike and disenchantment with Ed Garvey's leadership of the union began to mount.

As happened in the baseball strike of 1981, real pressure for settlement of the impasse occurred only when it became likely that the rest of the season would have to be forfeited if the strike continued much longer. Unlike the baseball strike, however, football player solidarity eventually showed signs of crumbling completely, with some players appearing on television to urge the others to return to play. Paul Martha, a former player and executive with the San Francisco Forty-Niners, made a last-ditch attempt to mediate the dispute. His efforts were successful because, by this time, the parties were willing to come to terms.

The players gave up their demands for a wage scale based on seniority, but achieved a total compensation package of $1.6 billion over five years with a $1.28 billion guarantee. There is little doubt that the owners won the fifty-seven-day strike. While the settlement appears generous, it is far less than the owners could have afforded, given substantial income from attendance and television. The continuation of the old system with little change for another five years made NFL franchises more profitable than ever.

Player Salaries

Salary Trends

Until the formation of the USFL, there was little reason for NFL teams to spend lavishly on player salaries. Except for playing in Canada, threatening to not play at all, and very limited opportunities for free agency, NFL players had no alternative to accepting the club's salary offer at terms favorable to the owner. Unlike other professional team sports in which team sizes are smaller and the value of personal performance is magnified, individual football players have less influence on overall team success. Stadiums are already filled to near capacity, and television revenues are guaranteed.

Table 3.2 shows average salaries in the NFL for selected years since 1967. In 1967 NFL players were paid significantly more than in any other professional sport, having been elevated as a result of the bidding wars between NFL and AFL teams. Over the years, football player salaries rose, but not nearly so fast as those of athletes in other sports. In 1982, however, as a result of higher salary minimums negotiated by the NFLPA and the renewed upward pressure from a competitive league, NFL salaries began to rise sharply again.

Table 3.2   Average NFL Salaries, 1967–85

Year	Average
1967	$ 25,000
1972	35,000
1977	55,288
1982	90,412
1983	112,967
1984	158,600
1985	190,000

Source: 1967, 1972, 1977 data from Ray Kennedy and Nancy Williamson, "Money: The Monster Threatening Sports," *Sports Illustrated*, 17 July 1978, 46. Data for 1982 to 1985 from the National Football League Players Association.

Football

The USFL influence on NFL salaries works two ways: NFL teams have to pay their present players more to keep them from jumping to the new league, and they must pay more to top players leaving college to sign them as draft choices, since these players may also be sought by the USFL. John Elway, a rookie in 1983, became the highest paid player in the NFL when he signed a five-year, $5 million contract with the Denver Broncos, and salaries of first-round draft choices in 1983 were up about 60 percent over 1982. In 1984 the highest NFL rookie contracts went to Irving Fryar of the New England Patriots ($3.4 million for four years) and Kenny Jackson of the Philadelphia Eagles ($3.3 million for four years). Rookie salaries were somewhat moderated in 1985 by the USFL's switch to a fall schedule and a glut of players competing for positions in the NFL. The richest rookie conract in 1985 went to Bernie Kosar of the Cleveland Browns, $5.2 million for five years.

Average salaries for the years from 1982 to 1984 are given by position in table 3.3. Quarterbacks were the highest paid, at $381,000, and punters were lowest at $92,000. In an interesting study of variables affecting pay by position, Ahlburg and Dworkin found that rates of return for "experience" were highest among the running backs.[10] Apart from seniority, other factors

Table 3.3   NFL Average Salaries by Position, 1982–84

Position	1984	1983	1982
Quarterbacks	$381,000	$223,000	$161,000
Running backs	269,000	127,000	96,000
Wide receivers	215,000	115,000	89,000
Defensive linemen	210,000	130,000	90,000
Linebackers	185,000	115,000	84,000
Offensive linemen	184,000	128,000	90,000
Tight ends	176,000	121,000	86,000
Defensive backs	151,000	117,000	79,000
Kickers	121,000	105,000	71,000
Punters	92,000	80,000	65,000

Source: National Football League Players Association.

Table 3.4   Percentage of Black Players in the NFL, 1969–84

Year	Percentage
1969	33.7
1979	48.8
1983	52.2
1984	52.0

Source: *Sports Illustrated*, 17 September 1984, 63.

explaining the pay levels of individual players in the NFL are the position played, draft round, and performance.

Professional football has been a source of economic advancement for blacks. The first black players in professional football were Kenny Washington and Woodie Strode, who signed with the Los Angeles Rams in 1946. For many years, the number of blacks on NFL rosters remained small, but by the mid-1960s their proportion began to become significant, and today they constitute a majority of NFL players. Table 3.4 shows the percentage of blacks in the NFL for selected years since 1969. Except for hockey, which has only a handful of black players, all major professional team sports have high proportions of blacks; the percentage of black players is highest in basketball, which also pays the highest average salaries of any team sport.

Salaries since the USFL

When Red Grange signed with the Chicago Bears in 1925, it gave the NFL a celebrity attraction that helped the infant league prosper. Joe Namath did the same for the AFL when he signed with the New York Jets. The USFL recognized the importance of employing big-name stars to enhance its public image, but its initial policy of holding salaries to no more than $1.6 million per club was not likely to attract many star players. A break from this policy came during the USFL's first year, when the New Jersey Generals signed Herschel Walker. Walker's contract was originally set for six years, but was renegotiated at $6 million for four years. Other big contracts were signed by Mike Rozier with the Pittsburgh Maulers at $3 million and by Marcus Dupree with the New Orleans Breakers at $6 million for five years. In what was reported as the richest contract in professional sports history, Steve Young agreed in 1984 to a "lifetime" contract with the Los Angeles Express providing payments of $40 million. Agent Leigh Steinberg was to receive an estimated $2 million for negotiating Young's contract. The USFL is a boon to agents, who benefit from competitive bidding and who may get double benefits from renegotiating contracts with NFL teams if the USFL folds.

Steve Young's contract, which was to run for forty-three years, raised questions about whether the $40 million obligation represented an inflated figure. Technically, the contract only committed Young to playing for four years for the team. During this period he was to receive annual salary, bonuses, and an interest-free loan, for a total of $5.9 million. The rest of the contract represented deferred payments totaling $34.5 million by the year 2027. The deferred payments, however, were to be financed by an annuity purchased by the Express. The entire annuity can be calculated to cost the team only about $2.5 million.[11] Thus, in terms of actual money spent by the team, the contract was more accurately described as a four-year $8.4 million deal, which included $5.9 million in direct compensation plus a $2.5 million annuity. In 1985, with the validity of Young's contract in doubt because of the team's financial difficulties, he bought out the contract and signed with the NFL's Tampa Bay club.

Attendance and television ratings for USFL games are far lower than in the NFL. Although USFL attendance increased by nearly 10 percent from 1983 to 1984, television ratings (on ABC) dropped from 6.0 to 5.5. USFL teams lost a total of about $20 million in the first year of operation,[12] and losses continued to mount to $80 million in 1984 with the signing of more star players to rich contracts. Early on, the NFL showed little concern about the rivalry. Its owners had seen competitors come and go before. But as USFL teams pirated more players from the NFL and signed more top college stars, NFL teams began to open their wallets to reverse the trend. The competition substantially cut the profits of NFL teams.

The wealthy businessmen who own USFL teams received an enormous amount of free publicity from signing players, which has probably titillated their egos and helped their outside enterprises. Yet it is questionable whether competition between the two leagues will continue for long. Football in the spring and early summer is simply not attractive to many sports fans, whose minds turn naturally to baseball in these seasons. Tradition is a big obstacle for the USFL to overcome, which explains why the league is planning to shift its schedule to the fall in 1986. The paucity of network television coverage is another factor, although the league's new three-year, $70 million cable deal with ESPN will help stem losses. One thing is certain: the longer the interleague rivalry continues, the more players will gain in higher salaries.

Antitrust Issues

The Sherman Act of 1890 is the principal antitrust law in America. It was passed by the federal government to control the growth of trusts, powerful business firms that engaged in monopolistic practices to stifle competition. The key language of this law that is applied to the regulation of business, including professional sports, is "Every contract, combination in the form of trust or otherwise on conspiracy in restraint of trade or commerce among the several states . . . is hereby declared illegal." The Sherman Act provides for treble damages in cases of violation of the law.

The NFL has an exemption from Congress that allows it to pool television rights without violation of the antitrust law. The merger between the NFL and AFL was also exempted. Apart from these exemptions, however, antitrust law has been applied to football in several instances, involving such issues as free agency, drafting of players, and movement of franchises.

Free Agency

Before 1976 professional football had the same kind of reserve system as other sports. That is, players entered into the game through drafting by single teams. Players signed standard contracts that bound them to their teams for their careers unless they were traded, sold, or put on waivers. There was hardly any freedom for players to initiate movement from one team to another.[13] Having only one choice of employer, players were in a weak bargaining position.

The first important legal case challenging the owners' control over players was *Radovich*, decided by the U.S. Supreme Court in 1957.[14] William Radovich had been a guard for the Detroit Lions. He contended that he had

77

been blacklisted by the NFL and prevented from earning a living in his profession. He charged the league with a conspiracy to monopolize and control professional football in violation of the Sherman Act of 1890. The Supreme Court's six-to-three decision did not award damages to Radovich, but it did establish the principle that professional football comes under the coverage of the antitrust laws because of the volume of interstate commerce involved in the sport. After this decision, the NFL tried to get Congress to give it a complete exemption from the antitrust laws, but such a law was not passed.

In 1962 a crack opened in the control of owners over players when R. C. Owens of the San Francisco Forty-Niners played out his option and signed a contract with the Baltimore Colts. The crack was temporarily repaired by the owners the following year by establishment of what became known as the Rozelle Rule. This rule allowed NFL commissioner Pete Rozelle to award compensation (players, draft choices, money) to a player's former team when he signed a contract with a new team. From 1963 to 1976, only four players played out their options and signed with other clubs—Pat Fischer, David Parks, Phil Olson, and Dick Gordon. In effect, the Rozelle Rule denied players the opportunity to sell their services to other teams. To sign a player who played out his option was risky because it was uncertain what penalty would be imposed on the club by the commissioner. For example, Dave Parks, an all-pro receiver for the San Francisco Forty-Niners, played out his option and signed with the New Orleans Saints. Commissioner Rozelle ordered the Saints to give up to the Forty-Niners their first-round draft choices in both 1968 and 1969. This was a very harsh penalty for the Saints.

A challenge to the Rozelle Rule was first made by Joe Kapp.[15] Kapp was a quarterback for the Minnesota Vikings, and when his contract expired, the club invoked its option clause for the 1969 season. Kapp then agreed to play for the New England Patriots in 1970, but did not sign a standard player contract with the Patriots. When he refused to sign such a contract for the following year, he was not allowed to play. His lawsuit sought damages from the NFL for terminating his playing career. Although the federal court rejected Kapp's claim that the Rozelle Rule was an illegal conspiracy to restrain trade and monopolize football in violation of the antitrust laws, it did find that the NFL's enforcement of the rule was too severe and caused undue hardship on the players.

In the *Mackey* case, a second court challenge was made to the Rozelle Rule under the antitrust laws.[16] John Mackey was a tight end for the Baltimore Colts and president of the NFLPA who alleged that the rule violated the Sherman Act by denying players an opportunity to contract freely for their services. The federal courts agreed with this contention, finding that the Rozelle Rule was an unreasonable restraint of trade because it acted as a prohibitive deterrent to player movement in the NFL.

With the decision in *Mackey*, NFL players were able to become free agents by playing out their option with the barrier of compensation penalty to their new team no longer in the way. The NFLPA, however, bargained away the rights won in the courtroom and locked itself into a new method of determining compensation payments for signing free agents. This provision, negotiated in the 1977 collective bargaining agreement, allowed scarcely more free agent mobility than the Rozelle Rule. The 1982 agreement liberalized free agency somewhat, but compensation penalties remained severe.

What finally broke the log jam was the opportunity for an NFL player to play out his option and then sign with a USFL club. In this case, compensation was not required because it was a separate league not bound by the contract between the NFL and NFLPA. The USFL presented a way of not only dodging the compensation bullet, but also of achieving a richer contract as a free agent. At the same time, a free agent NFL player would still be able to sign another contract with his NFL club, but at far higher pay because of the opportunity to jump leagues. One player, Billy Sims of the Detroit Lions, signed a contract with his NFL team and then tried to get out of it by signing two contracts with the USFL. (A bumper sticker appeared on automobiles in the Motor City saying "Honk if you have a contract with Billy.") After litigation, Sims wound up staying with the Lions.

NFL owners have some financial incentive to win and thus to bid for free agents who would further team success on the field. But in order for free agency to be successful in raising salaries, the draft would have to be eliminated and the revenue sharing scheme of the owners abolished.[17] Therefore, if gate receipts from playoffs went only to participating teams or if these teams received a larger share of playoff monies, the nexus between winning and revenues would be stronger.

NFL Draft

The NFL draft was challenged on antitrust grounds in the *Smith* case.[18] Yazoo Smith was a defensive back selected by the Washington Redskins as its number-one draft choice in 1968. He suffered a career-ending neck injury in the final game of that year. Smith's suit alleged that the draft denied him bargaining power and restricted him from obtaining contract provisions to protect his financial future in case of a disabling injury. In the meantime, while the case was being heard in the federal courts, the NFL changed the draft rules, so the case did not have an effect on the modified draft procedure. Nonetheless, the U.S. Court of Appeals found that the old draft procedure was illegal. Although the appellate court did not find a violation of the antitrust laws, it noted that the draft reduced competition by taking away opportunities for college players to market their talents. The U.S. District Court had earlier noted that one of the ways to decrease the anticompetitive influence of the NFL draft on college players was to reduce the number of selection rounds. This step was taken by the NFL to insulate itself from further judicial scrutiny.

When Herschel Walker signed with the USFL, other questions were raised about the draft. Before the Walker contract, the USFL indicated that it would follow the NFL's long-standing rule of not drafting players until they had completed four years of college football eligibility or until five years from the time that they enrolled in college. Since Walker was a college junior with another year of eligibility when he was signed, the USFL broke its own rule to secure him.

Then in 1984 a U.S. District Court overturned the USFL's rule on antitrust grounds. The rule was challenged by Bob Boris, a former punter at the University of Arizona, who sought to play in the USFL before his class had graduated. He signed with the Los Angeles Express when the USFL waived its eligibility rule for him, as it had done earlier with Walker. At the time of the suit, Boris had been cut by the Express and was playing for the Oklahoma Outlaws. Judge Laughlin Waters found that the rule constituted a group boycott and was a per se violation of the Sherman Act. Because this decision opened the door for other college underclassmen to be drafted by and sign with USFL clubs, it could turn out to be a landmark case. Even if the decision is later reversed on appeal, many players will already have signed contracts without completing eligibility requirements under the old rule.

Player draft rules provide a scheme that is beneficial to owners in the sense of allowing them to collude to keep salaries low by monopoly control over signings.[19] It may promote a more equal distribution of talent among teams because teams draft in reverse order of their place in league standings the year before. But it penalizes players for being talented because the very best go to the least successful teams. The USFL draft allows for territorial draft choices so that players can be retained in the regions where they played their college careers. It also allows teams to cooperate on the drafting of a particular player if they feel it is in the interest of the league. The Los Angeles Express, for instance, persuaded other teams not to draft Steve Young because if he signed in Los Angeles, the second-largest market in the USFL, the league would prosper by greater exposure. This kind of collusive arrangement was not a disservice to Young, but might prove so to other players. Such noncompetitive practices may mean that teams in the smaller markets may get fewer excellent players.

Restrictions like the draft do not exist in areas of the labor market other than sport. Advocates of the NFL rule prohibiting the drafting and signing of underclassmen note that players need a college education so that they can move on to other endeavors after their professional football careers. This argument has some merit, but it belies the fact that many college athletes matriculate in watered down curricula, and only about a third of NFL players have earned college degrees.[20] The NFL's drafting rules are far more restrictive than rules on player eligibility in any other major professional sport. Baseball and basketball, for example, permit drafting after high school, and hockey at age eighteen. The U.S. District Court decision on the USFL's rule probably signals the beginning of the end of the NFL's rule, which many observers agree is also a violation of the antitrust laws. In the absence of congressional intervention, it could be only a matter of time before large numbers of young players start going to the USFL and NFL after only two or three years of playing in college.

Franchise Movement

The movement of team franchises from one city to another can also raise antitrust issues. Al Davis, owner of the Oakland Raiders, sought permission under NFL rule 4.3 to relocate his franchise in Los Angeles. Always known as an innovative, farsighted, and successful owner, Davis was interested in Los Angeles because of a larger stadium facility and television market. Were the NFL to sign a contract with pay television in the future, the revenues might not be shared equally among teams, so teams in big television markets would get larger shares. But rule 4.3 prevented a team from relocating without a three-fourths vote of all teams. When Davis did not get the necessary votes, he went ahead with his plans to move the Raiders to Los Angeles anyway. When the NFL tried to block the move, Davis charged that rule 4.3 violated the antitrust laws. In 1982 a jury in U.S. District Court in Los Angeles decided that the NFL violated the Sherman Act by trying to prevent the Raiders from moving. The U.S. Court of Appeals in San Francisco upheld the jury verdict, and the U.S. Supreme Court declined without comment to hear the NFL's final appeal in 1984.[21]

Meanwhile, two other developments may yet return the Raiders to Oakland, although the probability that this will happen is very low. The city of Oakland has filed an eminent domain suit that, if successful, would allow the city to buy the Raiders as a civic asset. This is an unusual case in that eminent domain is ordinarily used by government agencies to seize property for freeways and other public works. In an aside to the main suit, the California Supreme Court found that maintenance of a sports franchise may be an appropriate municipal function for exercising eminent domain rights, thus clearing the way for the case to proceed on the issue of whether the city of Oakland can exercise this right in the matter of the Raiders.[22] The other development is legislation introduced in Congress to protect communities that support their franchises by allowing the NFL to disapprove relocation of franchises without running afoul of antitrust law. This would recognize the long and faithful support that the people of Oakland gave the Raiders and the important emotional and financial stake that the city has in the team.

Following Al Davis's lead, Baltimore Colts owner Robert Irsay moved his team to Indianapolis. This deprived another proud city with a long professional football tradition of its team. Commissioner Rozelle indicated that in view of the enormous expense of trying to stop Al Davis (estimated at about $50 million), the NFL would not oppose the move by Irsay. Thus the league seems to have entered into a "free agency" era for franchise movement.

USFL Suit

In October 1984 the USFL filed a $1.32 billion antitrust suit against the NFL, which is the largest lawsuit yet filed in professional sports. (The USFL seeks $440 million in damages, which under the Sherman Act would be tripled if the USFL prevails in the litigation.) The crux of this suit is the allegation that numerous predatory and unlawful actions were undertaken in a conspiracy by the NFL to perpetuate its monopoly power and prevent successful operation by a rival league. Named as an "involuntary co-conspirator" in the suit is ABC, the network on which USFL games are presented. A few months before the suit, ABC's initial $18 million, two-year contract with the league expired. The network had the option under this contract to pick up games in the 1985 season for $14 million and in 1986 for $18 million. It exercised its option for 1985. ABC was included in the litigation because it allegedly refused to negotiate in good faith on the 1985 option year renewal, failed to promote USFL games during its other programing, and made disparaging remarks about the USFL.

In its complaint against the NFL, the USFL alleged that the NFL (1) entered into long-term, exclusive agreements with stadium operators that froze out competitors, (2) exercised unfair control over the major television networks, with the objective of excluding the USFL from competitive programing, and (3) controlled the available pool of player talent by practices such as signing free agents to play for future seasons during the current season. If successful, the USFL suit would also break the NFL's network television and stadium contracts. Similar antitrust actions against the NFL in the past, by the American Football League and the World Football League, were unsuccessful.

Substance Abuse

Drug abuse has become a serious concern in professional team sports. Until recently, however, little effort was made to deal with the problem. Amphetamines, stimulants to the central nervous system, have long been part of the culture of football players. As we are frequently reminded by broadcasters, football is a game of emotion, and the team that reaches a higher level of emotional intensity is more likely to win. Players have also long relied on painkillers to enable them to play with minor injuries, and anabolic steroids are used by some football players to develop their muscles and gain strength.

Widespread use of amphetamines in football came to light in 1973, when it was estimated that between one-third and one-half of the players on the Washington Redskins team used the drug to get up for games.[23] Because amphetamines were sometimes distributed by team physicians and were otherwise easily available to players, the NFL for several years required that a bulletin be posted in locker rooms to the effect that it did not condone the use of pep pills and warned players against their use. The NFL also had security representatives make annual visits to teams to express its disapproval of drug misuse. Spot checks were occasionally made by security personnel, and a physician was hired by the league to evaluate bills of drug purchases submitted by teams. In 1974 Commissioner Rozelle fined the San Diego Chargers, its general manager, and eight of its players for improper use and distribution of drugs to the team. These measures for drug control, however, were primarily aimed at the use of amphetamines and other mild forms of abuse. More serious drug abuse problems involving possible criminal penalties had not emerged yet.

A public disclosure by Don Reese in 1982 brought to light widespread use of cocaine by football players. A former player for the New Orleans Saints, Reese was convicted for dealing in cocaine, and he revealed the considerable use of this drug by NFL players. Although there had been some earlier evidence of a cocaine problem among NFL players, players who disclosed their problems, such as Carl Eller of the Minnesota Vikings, were thought to be isolated cases. Few people realized the dimensions of cocaine use in football. Commissioner Rozelle had down-played the drug problem by taking the position that football players had no greater drug problem than does society. With Reese's disclosure, Commissioner Rozelle mounted a public relations campaign to express the NFL's concern and intention to take action.

The NFL's revised program emphasized education and rehabilitation. Players were informed of treatment programs and given counseling and warnings by officials of the Drug Enforcement Administration and the Federal Bureau of Investigation. Gene Upshaw of the NFLPA became active in talking with players about drug abuse, as did some team coaches. The centerpiece of the rehabilitation phase of the program was to send players who requested help to the Hazelden Clinic in Minnesota, with the NFL paying the bills and not disclosing names of players. But few players came forward to admit they had problems, and stories of cocaine use continued. According to a story in the *New York Daily News*, which was widely referenced in the media, cocaine was used by as many as 50 percent of NFL players, with about 20 percent qualifying as "hardcore" users.[24] Commissioner Rozelle responded that according to NFL security reports, the figures were exaggerated. Public pressure for action kept growing after five members of the Dallas Cowboys were investigated for suspected cocaine violations and Tony

Peters of the Washington Redskins was arrested and later imprisoned for acting as a go-between in a cocaine sale.

The NFL's drug policy acquired a punitive aspect when it became a law enforcement center as well as providing education and rehabilitation. Before the start of the 1983 season, the NFL suspended four players without pay for four games. Ross Browner and Pete Johnson of the Cincinnati Bengals had admitted in federal court to purchasing cocaine from a drug dealer; in separate incidents, E. J. Junior of the St. Louis Cardinals and Greg Stemrick of the New Orleans Saints had both pleaded no contest and were convicted on cocaine felony charges. None of the players was imprisoned. In his announcement of the suspensions, Rozelle noted,

NFL players occupy a unique position in the eyes of the public. They are objects of admiration and emulation by countless fans, particularly young people. Involvement with illegal drugs poses numerous risks to the integrity of professional football and the public's confidence in it. Thus, every player must adhere to certain standards of personal conduct both on and off the field. Every player agrees by his employment contract to not engage in activities detrimental to the sport.[25]

Under Ed Garvey, the NFLPA would probably have attacked Commissioner Rozelle for taking such harsh action against players, arguing double jeopardy because Rozelle imposed his own sentence after the players had been dealt with in court. By the time of the cocaine busts, however, Gene Upshaw had taken over as the union's executive director, and he took a noncombative stance on the issue. In any event, there was little the union could do because the collective bargaining agreement provides the commissioner with control over the integrity of the game, and players are subject to discipline under their individual contracts.

The NFL's drug control program is incorporated into the 1982 collective bargaining agreement. It is administered primarily by the Hazelden Clinic. An interesting feature of the agreement is that while club physicians may direct players to Hazelden for testing for chemical abuse, spot testing by the club or physician is specifically prohibited. With the NFL's program in place and precedent on punishment established, the cocaine problem in football may have reached a peak. But problems of abuse will continue and will require substantial attention to prevention and treatment.

As yet, the NFL's program does not have much in it for prevention of drug abuse, except insofar as it seeks to educate players on the issues. Cooperation by the NFLPA will help in this regard. Teams have varying individual programs that provide additional help in prevention and treatment, and coaches have become more sensitized to the problems (Coach Bill Walsh of the Forty-Niners has accompanied players to drug rehabilitation centers). It seems clear, however, that effective prevention will not occur unless stronger peer pressures against the use of cocaine develop among players.

4. Basketball

$\mathcal{F}$ew persons who watch professional basketball are not impressed with the grace, skill, and quickness of the magnificent athletes who play the game. Off the court, these players are motivated by the same economic objective as athletes in other major professional sports, to maximize their financial returns over short playing careers. As in other sports, players have formed a union, the National Basketball Players Association (NBPA), to promote their collective interests, and they are usually represented by outside agents in their individual salary negotiations with clubs. The NBPA has been active in legal affairs, helping to establish free agency for greater player mobility and bargaining power. The union confronts a league, the National Basketball Association (NBA) that bargains on behalf of team owners through the familiar multiemployer structure. Industrial relations in professional basketball have not had the prominent media exposure that baseball and football have. There has never been a strike by players, yet there are a number of interesting developments, many of which are unique to the sport.

Baseball had its forerunner in the game of rounders in England, the country that also developed football's predecessor, rugby. Hockey has Canadian origins. But basketball is a distinctly American game. It was the creation in 1891 of Dr. James Naismith, an instructor at a YMCA training school in Springfield, Massachusetts.[1] Naismith was asked by the director of the school to devise a game that would occupy the attention of a fractious group of physical education students. After some experimentation, he hit on the idea of nailing two peach baskets to the balcony of the gymnasium. The object was to throw a ball into the basket, and the players were not allowed to run with the ball or use roughhouse tactics. A ladder was used to retrieve the ball. By 1912 an open net was used. Colleges took up the game, and the YMCA did much to promote it. Although the game changed substantially over the years, twelve of the original thirteen rules laid down by Naismith still survive.

Professional basketball began in 1898 with the formation of the National Basketball League. It folded after the 1902–3 season. Numerous other leagues were established in the early years, but it was not until the American Basketball League (ABL) started play in 1925 that something of a lasting foundation was laid. The ABL initially had nine teams, including the original Celtics who played their home games in New York (two of the stars of this team were Nat Holman and Joe Lapchick, who later became renowned coaches). But the ABL and other early leagues were poorly organized and managed. Players rarely had binding contracts and would jump back and forth between teams. Fan interest was minimal. A more stable league format was created when the National Basketball League began in 1937 and the Basketball Association of America in 1946. In 1949 these leagues merged to form the National Basketball Association, which continues today as the major professional league.

Economics of Basketball

The economics of professional basketball appear healthy on the surface, but a variety of circumstances in recent years have hurt profitability and called into question whether the game will continue as one of the major professional team sports in America.

NBA basketball is in a relatively favorable position to be packaged for spectators. With the demise of the ABA, there is no rival league to dilute fan appeal and drive salaries upward. There are considerable opportunities for exposing the sport to potential spectators, with a regular season schedule of eighty-two games plus extended playoffs and twenty-three teams operating in markets that extend to nearly all of the large population centers of the nation. Moreover, the game presents an attractive product for television. It has a compact playing area, few players to follow, and a highly visible ball. Although there is some overlap with the seasons for other sports, product competition during the winter months is not extensive. With only twelve players on a team, high salaries are justified because relatively few players must be paid.

Professional basketball teams have three major assets: the right to present games in a particular geographic area, player contracts, and access to an arena for staging games.[2] These are essentially contractual agreements that protect teams from competition. Profitability is determined by a number of factors, among them the inherent attraction of the game. Professional basketball has a constant flow of new, exciting players coming into the game who have already developed strong public recognition during their college careers, but the large number of games played and frequent travel sap players' vitality. Perhaps many fans have the perception that NBA games do not get interesting until the closing minutes, when players go all out to win, because it is difficult to maintain a fast pace over the entire game during the long season.

The financial success of individual teams depends primarily on the demand for games in the team's home city, the team's success, costs of operation, the club's tax liability, and how efficiently the franchise is managed. The greater the population in the team's home area and the larger the arena size, the greater will be the potential market and gate receipts. Like other professional sports, basketball has its rich-poor dichotomy, with teams in New York and Los Angeles having great market advantages over teams in Utah and Sacramento. A team's win-loss record is important in attracting fans and justifying higher ticket prices, and because the addition of a single superstar player can make a significant difference in the team playing success, top free agents are in great demand. When owners try to gain an edge by raising salaries, the costs of operation can rise quickly. In the late 1970s and early 1980s, the increases in gross income did not come close to keeping pace with the increases in player salaries. Several teams consistently lost money during this period. In a classic case of poor management, Ted Stepien, owner of the Cleveland Cavaliers, paid enormous salaries to free agents and traded away draft choices only to acquire a team with players of limited

---

Table 4.1   Average Attendance at NBA Games, 1967–85

Season	Attendance
1967–68	5,967
1971–72	8,061
1972–73	8,396
1973–74	8,479
1974–75	9,339
1975–76	10,179
1976–77	10,974
1977–78	10,947
1978–79	10,822
1979–80	11,017
1980–81	10,021
1981–82	10,567
1982–83	10,220
1983–84	10,620
1984–85	11,141

Source: National Basketball Association.

---

skills. When he finally sold the team, the NBA voted to allow the new owners to regain four first-round draft choices in an effort to revitalize the wrecked franchise.

Average attendance at NBA games has not been strong during the past decade (see table 4.1), although 1984–85 was encouraging in that attendance set a record high. The weakness of attendance in recent years is explained by various factors. One is that college basketball has increased in relative popularity, draining fans from the professional game. High ticket prices have discouraged many fans. Also, indoor soccer has emerged as a competitor to basketball.

Television

Although basketball is well suited to television coverage, it has always ranked a poor third to football and baseball in terms of television ratings.

The first nationally televised professional basketball game, between the New York Knickerbockers and Boston Celtics, was shown on NBC in 1954. The owners recognized the importance of television exposure to expanding interest in and profitability of the game, and they began to negotiate network and local television agreements. A three-year agreement was reached with CBS to televise thirty-eight games each season, beginning in the 1973–74 season. In 1976, this agreement with CBS was extended for two years in a $10.5 million deal arranged by Commissioner Lawrence O'Brien.

Beginning in the 1982–83 season, a four-year $88 million television agreement with CBS paid each team about $1 million a season. In addition, each team received another $240,000 annually from league contracts with the USA and ESPN cable networks, plus anywhere from $100,000 to $1 million from local television agreements, either on free television or cable.[3] National cable television revenues doubled for the 1984–85 and 1985–86 seasons under a contract with WTBS, the Atlanta-based network, to show fifty-five regular season and twenty playoff games each year. But these television revenues are minuscule compared with those for football and baseball. The number of basketball games shown on national television is also far fewer. More NBA teams are entering into local cable television agreements, but this source may not produce the hoped-for salvation because what is not popular on national free television may not generate much interest on pay television either.

Structure of Employment

NBA and the ABA

The NBA had seventeen teams in its inaugural season, but lost six teams for the second season and was down to only eight teams by 1957. Since then, the league has steadily expanded to twenty-three teams in 1985–86, each of which plays an eighty-two-game schedule. There is also a good number of postseason playoff games, with eligibility determined by placement among the top sixteen best won-lost records. The NBA is a joint venture. Most clubs are owned by corporations, but authority is exercised by a single dominant owner who is usually the majority stockholder. Club owners join together to make policy decisions on rules and other matters of common interest through the board of governors of the NBA. The league also has a labor relations committee, composed of owners, which is primarily responsible for collective bargaining.

After the merger of the two leagues to form the NBA in 1949, there was no serious threat to its hegemony over professional basketball. In the 1960s, however, two leagues were formed that caused competition for acquisition of players and fan attention and provided stimulus to NBA salaries. The first of these rivals, the American Basketball League (ABL), was formed in 1961 by Abe Saperstein, owner of the Harlem Globetrotters.[4] Despite such innovations as awarding three points for field goals initiated from more than twenty-five feet from the basket, the ABL never really caught on among fans and had very limited television exposure. After only one full season and part of another it collapsed. Before the start of the ABL's truncated second season, the best team in the league, the Cleveland Pipers, was absorbed into the NBA. Losses to the league's eight teams were estimated at $1.5 million in the first season, and no team was profitable when the league folded. About one hundred players lost their jobs.

In 1967 a more formidable rival for the NBA emerged. The American Basketball Association (ABA) was far better financed and organized than the ABL. Creation of the league was largely the work of Gary Davidson, a maverick sports entrepreneur who also founded competitive sports leagues in football and hockey. The commissioner of the new league was George Mikan, formerly a great player with the Minneapolis Lakers. A key ABA strategy was to avoid head-to-head competition with NBA teams by establishing as many ABA franchises as possible in non-NBA cities. The league began play in the 1967–68 season with teams in Anaheim, Dallas, Denver, Houston, Indianapolis (called Indiana), Louisville (called Kentucky), Minneapolis (called Minnesota), New Jersey, New Orleans, Oakland, and Pittsburgh. Only three of these franchises—New Jersey, Anaheim, and Oakland—competed for spectators with teams in nearby NBA cities (New York, Los Angeles, and San Francisco). Another tactic to preserve the financial strength of ABA teams was to avoid bidding wars for players with NBA teams. This policy did not hold for long, however, since ABA teams soon began to draft and sign top college players. To spice up play, the ABA had three-point field goals (from more than twenty-five feet), a thirty-second shot clock, and a resplendent red-white-and-blue basketball.

Many of the initial ABA players were NBA rejects or marginal players who jumped leagues. An exception was the brilliant forward Rick Barry, who went from the NBA's San Francisco Warriors to the Oakland Oaks of the ABA. In later seasons, several other outstanding NBA players jumped leagues, including Zelmo Beatty, Billy Cunningham, and Dave Bing. Some talented players—for example, David Thompson, Dan Issel, Bobby Jones, and Artis Gilmore—also joined the ABA's teams directly from college, with more coming as the league became better established. What gave the ABA a leg up on the NBA in attracting potential superstars was that the new league did not adhere to the NBA rule of waiting until a player's college class had graduated before making him eligible for drafting. Thus the ABA picked off such plums as Moses Malone, who signed out of high school, and Julius ("Dr. J") Erving, George McGinnis, and George Gervin, who all left college early. Another interesting star in the ABA was Connie Hawkins, who was at first barred from the NBA because of a collegiate gambling scandal.

The ABA struggled through the first year without a television contract. In ensuing years local TV contracts were signed with ABA teams, but the big national network coverage never materialized. Nevertheless, the ABA enjoyed a measure of respectability, and many observers felt that overall its players nearly achieved parity with those in the NBA. After its first season, league players formed the American Basketball Association Players Association in Denver. Larry Jones of the Denver Rockets was its first president. The ABA union never became a dominant force against the owners. Its most significant accomplishment appears to have been a licensing and merchandising agreement with the league and Metro-Goldwyn-Mayer to arrange deals with companies in the food, toy, and other industries for use of the ABA name.

The opening round in the bidding war between the leagues began in 1968, when the NBA stole a march on its rival by holding an early draft for first-round choices. Competition between the leagues for players caused a tremendous surge in salaries, making basketball players by far the highest paid professional team athletes. It was estimated that owners of ABA teams lost $50 million during the nine years of the league's existence,[5] and the competition also cut deeply into NBA profits. After just two years of bidding wars, the rival leagues realized that further competition would be difficult to sustain.

In 1969 officials of the leagues began talks directed at merger or, at the least, establishment of a common draft. The NBPA quickly announced its vigorous opposition to any kind of collusion between the leagues, arguing that a merger or common draft would restrict a player's ability to earn a living. But after several months of discussions, ABA owners agreed to pay an indemnity of $11 million to merge with the NBA and to have limited interleague play, playoffs, and an all-star game between the two leagues.[6] This prompted the NBPA to file an antitrust suit in federal court to stop the merger as well as to challenge the draft, uniform contract, and the reserve clause that tied a player to one team within the NBA. A temporary restraining order and later a preliminary injunction were issued by the federal courts to prevent the merger pending determination on the merits of the suit.

Despite the injunction, the leagues proceeded with plans to merge, and in 1970 both voted in favor of merger, subject to approval by Congress. Congress had approved a merger of the National and American Football Leagues in 1966, but at that time there was no opposition from the players of either league. Thus the basketball leagues, in the face of opposition from NBA players, sought congressional exemption from the antitrust laws to allow them to merge in order to stop the bidding war by establishing a common draft and arrangements for the signing of free agents. United States Senator Sam J. Ervin, Jr., called for a careful review of the antitrust issue in basketball and sponsored legislation applying the Sherman Act to professional sports.[7] This legislation was not enacted by Congress, however, so the problems continued.

The potential merger of the ABA and NBA was complicated by the fact that each league negotiated with a union representing its players. With separate bargaining units, the question arose as to whether the leagues needed approval from both players' associations in order to establish a common draft. If the merger was approved, the players would clearly suffer because competition for their services would be eliminated. Had Congress granted approval for exemption from the antitrust laws, the merger of the leagues would have gotten around the meddlesome players. But the failure of Congress to sanction the merger placed the determination of the issue back in the hands of the courts, where it was to languish for several years. During this period the merger agreement between the leagues expired, and the leagues awaited the outcome of litigation before resuming efforts to merge.

When the legal issues barring a merger were finally removed, the door was opened for resumption of talks. In June 1976 the NBA and ABA consolidated into a twenty-two-team league. Four of the six surviving teams in the

ABA were absorbed into the NBA and began play in the 1976–77 season. These teams—New York Nets, Indiana Pacers, Denver Nuggets, and San Antonio Spurs—were each required to pay $3.2 million in cash to the NBA. In addition, the Nets were required to indemnify the New York Knickerbockers by cash payments over several years for moving into their territory.

The Kentucky Colonels and Utah Rockies were left out of the merger and were paid about $3 million each by the four teams that were accepted in the NBA. Kentucky and Utah players were dispersed in a special draft involving all twenty-two teams. Because they had the worst record in the league, the Chicago Bulls had first choice in the dispersal draft of twenty players and selected Artis Gilmore from Kentucky. Other outstanding players available through this draft were Moses Malone and Maurice Lucas. Although numerous league and team officials played an important role in the merger, the principal architects were Larry O'Brien, commissioner of the NBA, and David DeBusschere, commissioner of the ABA.

The Commissioner

The NBA commissioner, who holds a position formerly known as president of the NBA, is influential in labor relations. The first president of the league was Maurice Podoloff, who is credited with holding the league together in the difficult early years. In the infancy of the NBA, the most visible labor relations function of the president was to uphold the integrity of the game by investigating charges of gambling by players. Podoloff was succeeded as president in 1963 by Walter Kennedy, former mayor of Stamford, Connecticut. When Kennedy retired as commissioner in 1975, he was replaced by Lawrence F. O'Brien. At the time O'Brien was chosen by the owners, the NBA was embroiled in litigation over the proposed merger with the ABA and was active in congressional lobbying for antitrust law exemption. He seemed a perfect choice for the job because of his previous political experience as campaign manager for John F. Kennedy, Lyndon B. Johnson, and Hubert H. Humphrey and his service as national chairman of the Democratic party and as postmaster general.

Larry O'Brien proved to be a great leader during a very hectic period of the NBA, but not always in the way the owners wanted. He took a more sympathetic stand toward players' rights than was expected, although he was a strict disciplinarian on matters like player fighting and drug abuse.

O'Brien's major accomplishments were (1) resolution of an antitrust suit by players, (2) signing of three collective bargaining agreements that were among the most progressive in professional sports, (3) finalizing the merger with the ABA that resulted in the addition of four teams to the NBA, (4) negotiating major television contracts, and (5) instigation of a new drug control policy. When O'Brien resigned in 1983 he was succeeded as commissioner by David J. Stern. Stern had begun service with the NBA in 1967 as an attorney with the New York law firm that represented the league. In 1978 he became the NBA's general counsel and later an executive vice president for business and legal affairs. Stern worked closely with O'Brien over the years and was O'Brien's choice for the commissioner's post.

Players and Their Union

There are about three hundred players in the NBA. Nearly all of them are recruited from colleges, and NBA rosters are dominated by black players. In 1954 only about 5 percent of the league's players were black; by 1962 the percentage had risen to 30 percent and by 1970 to 57 percent.[8] In 1985 about 75 percent of the players on NBA rosters were black, a larger proportion than in any professional sport.

In the early years, professional basketball was segregated. The greatest black team was the Renaissance Big Five, organized in Harlem in 1922. The Rens, as they were popularly known, played against the best all-white teams in the 1930s and were considered the best team in the nation.[9] Another successful early black team was the Harlem Globetrotters, known primarily today for their clowning techniques that delight fans.

Baseball was the first major professional sport to break the color line when Jackie Robinson played for the Brooklyn Dodgers in 1947. Three years later, Chuck Cooper became the first black player in the NBA, signing with the Boston Celtics out of Duquesne University. In 1966 basketball became the first sport to employ a black coach when player Bill Russell succeeded Arnold ("Red") Auerbach as coach of the Boston Celtics, and since then other black players, such as Lennie Wilkins and Alvin Attles and K. C. Jones, have coached NBA teams. A black lawyer, Simon Gourdine, served as deputy commissioner in the NBA.

Various factors contribute to the prominence of blacks in professional basketball. Unlike such sports as golf or tennis, where economic constraints have prevented high black participation, basketball is a playground game that is readily accessible to most youths. Open university admission policies have given blacks greater opportunity to play at the college level. The NBA not only encouraged black players to participate through its draft but also protected them from racial harassment; for example, in 1959 the NBA board of governors established a policy to insulate black players from embarrassment stemming from segregated housing and dining facilities.[10] Formation of the rival ABA created additional jobs in basketball and unprecedented opportunities for black players.

The National Basketball Players Association (NBPA) was formed in 1954 by Bob Cousy, a star player for the Boston Celtics. He was assisted by his close friend and insurance agent, Joseph P. Sharry, who served as secretary-treasurer. Cousy selected an outstanding player from each team to serve as the initial player representatives. When its grievances were ignored for two years by president Maurice Podoloff, the NBPA threatened coercive action. There were rumors of a strike if the league did not recognize the association. Unable to get satisfaction from Podoloff, Cousy met with a representative of the American Guild of Variety Artists to consider affiliation with this labor union. Podoloff indicated that he was not opposed to the players organizing but felt that their association should be limited to players only.[11] In response to the players' threats, Podoloff invited their representatives to a joint meeting with the owners in 1957. Recognition was granted the NBPA at this meeting.[12]

After its recognition by the owners, the NBPA seemed to lose its vitality and cohesiveness. Organization was poor because there was no constitution or bylaws, and meetings were infrequent. This lack of organization as well as a shortage of funds made it difficult to mount a sustained membership drive, and no affiliation with another labor union was accomplished. Then in 1962 the players hired attorney Lawrence Fleisher as general counsel. Fleisher undertook a spirited organization campaign and tightened up the operation of the NBPA so that it could stand as a strong union without outside affiliation. He confronted the owners as an antagonist. With strike threats and a majority of the players behind him, Fleisher began to achieve significant gains. Unlike the executive directors in baseball and football, Fleisher currently serves only part time in his position. He also represents players as an agent in individual salary negotiations, like the head of the hockey players' union.

Basketball

Early Agreements

A major confrontation between the NBPA and owners in 1964 resulted in the establishment of a player pension plan. For several years the players had been trying to achieve pensions in talks with owners and the league president, and in 1962 the owners had forwarded a specific pension plan to Tom Heinsohn of the Boston Celtics, who succeeded Cousy as president of the union. Implementation of the plan was delayed, however, because Heinsohn did not realize that the owners' proposal had to be either accepted or rejected.[13] When Heinsohn and player representatives later expressed desire to put the pension plan into effect in meetings with league president Walter Kennedy, they were frustrated by stalling tactics. The matter came to a head when players threatened to boycott the 1964 all-star game and caused the game to be delayed by several minutes. This forced the owners to guarantee that they would take action to implement the pension plan.

The NBPA again threatened a strike over pension issues in 1967. This time the players said they would strike the championship playoffs and file for certification with the National Labor Relations Board as a labor union if their demands for increases in pension plan contributions were not met. The players sought an increase in pension payments to $600 a month at age sixty-five for players with ten years service, which they argued would bring them up to levels found in baseball and football. Shortly before the playoffs were to begin, the owners capitulated on the pension demands. In addition, the players won a new medical and insurance program, elimination of games played immediately before and after the all-star game, and limitation of the regular schedule to eighty-two games. The 1967 collective bargaining agreement was the first in all of professional sports.

In 1968 an agreement was signed by league president Kennedy and the new president of the NBPA, Oscar Robertson, to increase pay for rookies and veteran players. The following year, the players threatened to strike over the proposed merger between the NBA and ABA, contending that the merger would violate the antitrust laws. This dispute resulted in extensive litigation in the courts. In 1970, salary minimums, monies for the playoff pool, and meal allowances were increased after negotiations between the NBA commissioner and the NBPA. Before 1971, the Uniform Player's Contract could be unilaterally renewed with a 25 percent salary reduction. In 1971 this provision was changed so that renewal was at the same salary the player received in the preceding year of his contract. It was not until 1973 that the first comprehensive agreement was negotiated between the owners and players. In this three-year agreement the pattern of increasing minimum salaries, playoff shares, and pensions was continued. But many items that were the subject of individual agreement in the past were folded into one contract, and new items, such as arbitration, made their initial appearance in a contract.

When the 1973 agreement expired, negotiations were complicated by the antitrust suit of the players against the NBA-ABA merger. Over a period of several months, only one fruitless negotiating session was held. There was rumor of players not attending training camps as a protest to lack of progress, but the players reported as usual. It was not until the courtroom battle over the proposed merger was resolved that the parties were able to come up with a replacement agreement.

Player Salaries

Teams will make money if they pay players less than the contribution that their skills make to team revenues and will lose money if they pay players more than they bring in. That so many basketball teams have reported operating losses in recent years indicates that they have been paying out too much in salaries. In 1967 only about 30 percent of gross revenues went for players' salaries; by 1972 the percentage had risen to 66 percent and in 1977 to 70 percent.[14] By 1983 nearly three-quarters of revenues were allocated to salaries. During this period salaries rose dramatically in the NBA, making players the highest paid group in any sport (see table 4.2).

Two principal factors have led to surges in NBA salaries, the competition with the ABA that ignited salaries in the late 1960s and the removal of the need to provide compensation for the signing of free agents, which began in 1981. This points up the fact that change in player salaries is very different in situations of open competition for players. Owners have less control over competition from rival leagues. If they are too complacent and do not match salary levels offered in the market created by owners in the other league, their own survival is threatened. Although free agency poses a less serious threat in that owners can tacitly agree to keep from bidding against each other for players, there always seems to be at least one owner who refuses to

---

Table 4.2   Average Salaries in the NBA, 1967–86

Season	Average Salary
1967–68	$ 20,000
1972–73	90,000
1977–78	143,000
1979–80	173,000
1980–81	189,000
1981–82	218,000
1982–83	246,000
1983–84	275,000
1984–85	340,000
1985–86	395,000

Source: Data for 1967–78 from Ray Kennedy and Nancy Williamson, "Money: The Monster Threatening Sports," Sports Illustrated, 17 July 1978, 46. For 1979–83, data from David DuPree, "NBA: Red Ink and a Bleak Future," Washington Post, 15 March 1983, D4. Data for 1983–84 from Sports Illustrated, 2 July 1984, 14; and 1984–85 and 1985–86 estimated by the author from various sources.

---

go along, such as Ted Stepien, who established the early pattern for free agents in 1981, and Harold Katz, owner of the Philadelphia 76ers who in 1982 signed free-agent Moses Malone to a six-year contract for a total of $13.2 million. As it turned out, Malone was a good investment for Katz since 76ers' attendance rose significantly and the team won the NBA championship in Malone's first year with the club. But big contracts create a ripple effect that justifies higher salaries for other players, who may turn out to be poor investments.

Table 4.3 shows the highest paid basketball players in the 1985–86 season. Some of these contracts provide for substantial deferred payments after a player has left the game, the most extreme case being Earvin ("Magic") Johnson of the Lakers who signed a $25 million contract for twenty-five years. At the time Johnson's contract was signed, teams in the NBA were estimated to owe between $80 million and $90 million in deferred payments to current and former players.[15] As a result of the Johnson contract and the mounting deferred payment obligations, NBA owners agreed to establish a seventy-thirty rule, meaning that a player must get 70 percent of his contract up front in cash within a period defined by the life of the contract plus two

Table 4.3   NBA's Highest Paid Players, 1985–86

Player, Team	Annual Salary (in millions)
Earvin Johnson, Los Angeles	$2.5
Moses Malone, Philadelphia	2.125
K. Abdul-Jabbar, Los Angeles	2.03
Larry Bird, Boston	1.8
Patrick Ewing, New York	1.5
Jack Sikma, Seattle	1.2
Mitch Kupchak, Los Angeles	1.15
Otis Birdsong, New Jersey	1.075
Ralph Sampson, Houston	1.066
Julius Erving, Philadelphia	1.0
Kevin McHale, Boston	1.0

Source: National Basketball Association.

years after his last playing year. Only 30 percent of the payment can be deferred beyond this period. Johnson's contract has since been renegotiated.

Antitrust Issues

Unlike baseball, which enjoys special immunity, basketball comes under the purview of the antitrust laws. In *Washington Professional Basketball Corp. v. National Basketball Association*, a U.S. District Court found that the business of professional basketball is conducted on an interstate basis.[16] When this is coupled with the sale of rights to televise and broadcast games, the sport comes under the "trade or commerce among the several states" language of the Sherman Act.

Perpetual Reserve Clause

Although the reserve clause in basketball was not struck down until the 1975 case *Robertson* v. *National Basketball Association*,[17] court decisions in the 1960s backed away from the notion that the reserve clause had perpetual application. In the first of these cases, Richard Barnett played the 1960–61 season with the Syracuse Nationals of the NBA. Although Barnett's contract with the Nationals was a uniform contract that enabled the club to renew it for one year, he signed a contract for the 1961–62 season with the Cleveland Pipers of the ABL. Suing to stop Barnett from playing for the Pipers, the Nationals contended that although Barnett did not sign a contract with them for 1961–62, an oral agreement was reached.[18] The court found strong support for this contention because Barnett admitted requesting a salary advance from the club. Barnett, on the other hand, alleged that the contract with the Nationals was a restraint of trade in violation of the law.

The Court of Common Pleas of Ohio, finding for the Nationals, noted that professional basketball requires regulations for the protection of the business, public, and players. So long as these regulations are reasonable, as they were determined to be in this case, there is no violation of the law on restraint of trade. Interestingly, the court applied a test of reasonableness rather than automatically binding Barnett to the Nationals because of the reserve clause.

In a similar case, Louis Hudson, a player who tried to jump from the NBA's St. Louis Hawks to the ABA's Minnesota team, was held to be bound by his contract with the Hawks.[19] Again, the court found a special circumstance, in this case the fact that the Minnesota team did not have clean hands in its dealings with Hudson. As in *Barnett*, however, the result was that the player was not allowed to jump leagues.

In the *Barry* case, which presents some unique twists and turns, the player who tried to jump leagues eventually made it from the NBA to the ABA. The controversy concerned whether Rick Barry would play basketball for the Washington Capitols of the ABA or the San Francisco Warriors of the NBA.[20] In 1966 Barry signed a one-year contract with the Warriors that contained a reserve clause. The Warriors chose to exercise their option to get Barry to play for the 1967–68 season. Meanwhile, in 1967 Barry signed a three-year contract with the Oakland Oaks of the ABA. This prompted the Warriors to sue Barry to enforce their contract rights to his services. The California Court of Appeal held that the Warriors could stop Barry from playing for anyone else until September 30, 1968.[21] Even though Barry had not signed for the Warriors in 1967–68, the club had the option of renewing the contract for one year. As a result of this litigation, Barry did not play for anyone in 1967–68.

Barry began his ABA career in the 1968–69 season, playing for the Oakland Oaks. In 1969 the Oaks were sold and became the Washington Capitols. Because Barry had a three-year contract with the Oaks, he was part of the assets the new owners acquired. Immediately after the sale of the Oaks, however, Barry signed a five-year contract to play for the Warriors again. The U.S. Court of Appeals, affirming the district court, found that Barry was obligated to fulfill his contract with the Capitols. Barry had sought to invoke the clean-hands doctrine against the Capitols, contending that since he was not really free to play for the Oaks back in 1968, the Capitols, as the Oaks' transferee, lacked clean hands. Barry was thus trying to have it both ways, with the degree of his freedom depending on his own convenience. The court dismissed this unheroic argument by noting that it is difficult to imagine that someone who signed as many conflicting contracts as Barry would not be aware that the franchise might fail or be transferred to another city. So Barry was obligated to play for the Capitols, which he did until the ABA merged with the NBA. Then he returned to the Warriors.

Hardship Rule

Basketball was the first sport in which judicial mandate required modification of a rule prohibiting the signing of college players until four years after high school graduation. A similar rule in football was struck down by the courts in 1984. The controversy in basketball began in 1969 when Spencer Haywood signed a contract to play for the Denver Rockets of the ABA.[22] At the time, Haywood was too young to play in the ABA, but the league made an exception to the rule for him by waiving its application on hardship grounds. Early in the 1970–71 season, a dispute arose between Haywood and the Rockets about his contract. He stopped playing for that team and signed a contract with the Seattle Supersonics of the NBA. The NBA commissioner disapproved this contract because it violated section 2.05 of the NBA's bylaws, which stated,

A person who has not completed high school or who has completed high school but has not yet entered college, shall not be eligible to be drafted as a Player until four years after his original high school class has been graduated. . . . Similarly, a person who has entered college but is no longer enrolled, shall not be eligible to be drafted or to be a Player until the time when he would have first become eligible had he remained enrolled in college.[23]

103

The U.S. District Court ruled that the NBA did not provide "procedural safeguards" for an individual to contest his exclusion under section 2.05. It therefore determined that the NBA's rule was a violation of the Sherman Act. After the court decision, the NBA settled the suit by fining the Supersonics $200,000, and because of the settlement, the decision of the district court was not appealed. A further result of the litigation was that the NBA modified its rule to permit hardship cases among college players to be signed by its teams: players must prove hardship based on financial condition, family, academic record or lack of it, and ability to obtain employment in another field. As a practical matter, proving hardship has not been difficult for college underclassmen who want to sign with the NBA.

Screening of Owners

Although one might assume that transfer of ownership of a professional sports team is exclusively in the hands of the buyer and seller, transfer of franchise ownership requires approval by vote of the other owners. This authorization requirement allows owners to screen potential buyers in order to keep undesirable persons such as known criminals from becoming owners.

But whether a league can arbitrarily keep out any potential owner presents an interesting antitrust issue. In *Levin* v. *National Basketball Association*, the plaintiffs were two businessmen who had an agreement to buy the Boston Celtics of the NBA.[24] Action by the NBA Board of Governors was needed for transfer of ownership, with an affirmative vote of three-quarters of the owners. When the plaintiffs applied for approval of the transfer, they were turned down because they were friendly with Sam Schulman, owner of the Seattle Supersonics, who had given other NBA owners problems in the past. It was feared that the plaintiffs, if they gained ownership rights, would side with Schulman on future matters and cause trouble. When they were turned down for ownership, they brought suit charging violation of the antitrust laws. A U.S. District Court dismissed the charge, noting that antitrust laws protect competition, not individual competitors. Exclusion of the plaintiffs by the board of governors was found to not have an anticompetitive intent or effect and to cause no public injury.

Robertson Case

The most significant litigation in basketball is the *Robertson* case.[25] This case was filed in 1970 as a class action on behalf of all players by several former and current NBA players who had been team player representatives when the suit began. Leading the litigants was Oscar Robertson, who was perhaps the best guard to play the game during his career with the Cincinnati Royals and Milwaukee Bucks. The players charged that the reserve clause, uniform player contract, and college draft all violated the antitrust laws. They also sought to prevent the NBA from merging with the ABA. According to the players, the control of players through the draft and uniform contract was a conspiracy in restraint of trade that violated the Sherman Act. If a player refused to sign another uniform contract and sought to negotiate with another NBA club, he would be subject to a boycott or blacklisting. If such a negotiation occurred, the offending team was subject to a penalty by the NBA. All of this, argued the players, allowed the NBA to enforce their combination to monopolize and restrain trade. They charged that a merger between the NBA and ABA would eliminate what little competition existed for players' services.

In a threshold challenge, the NBA charged that the U.S. District Court lacked jurisdiction to decide the case, arguing that the NLRB had primary jurisdiction since matters within the scope of the National Labor Relations Act were involved. The court rejected this argument, finding that the antitrust issues involved in the case were not within the "special competence" of the NLRB and that therefore the federal court should appropriately decide the case.

Next, the NBA argued that it was protected from the antitrust laws by the so-called labor exemption: that is, that federal labor law encourages collective bargaining for resolving labor disputes, and as a result of this process, the interests of the individual employee must be subordinate to the collective interests of all. The court also rejected this argument, noting that the labor exemption applies only to labor or union activities, not to the activities of employers. It found that the threat employer restraints posed to the ideals of free competition outweighed the need to maintain the labor-management relationship. Moreover, reasoned the court, since the restraints were non-mandatory subjects of bargaining and were imposed unilaterally by the NBA, the labor exemption could not be used to achieve immunity from the antitrust laws. Even if the subjects were mandatory, the court would still not allow immunity because there had been no bona fide, arm's-length bargaining on the subjects.

Finding no acceptable defense by the NBA, the court determined that the draft, uniform contract, and reserve clause were a per se violation of the

Sherman Act and thus illegal. The court also found that the NBA-ABA merger would have the effect of restraining trade by eliminating competition between the two leagues for college players and preventing players from jumping leagues. Despite the decision in *Robertson*, the question of damages for the players as well as the practical effect of the decision on future labor relations arrangements remained open.

In 1976 a settlement was reached on the remaining *Robertson* case issues when the NBA and NBPA negotiated a new collective bargaining agreement. The owners agreed to pay $4.5 million in damages to about five hundred players, plus an additional $1 million for the players' legal fees. Apart from the monetary settlement, the 1976 agreement had four key features: (1) beginning with the 1976–77 season, the option clause would be eliminated from all nonrookie player contracts; (2) beginning in 1980 and continuing through the 1986–87 season, a right-of-first-refusal system was established, under which a player whose contract has expired and who receives an offer from another team can be retained by his original team if that team matches the offer; (3) the old compensation arrangement, i.e., teams that sign free agents must give up players, draft choices, cash, or some combination as compensation, as determined by the commissioner, remained in effect until the end of the 1980–81 season; and (4) the college draft remained in effect, except that if a player chose not to sign with the club that drafted him, he was eligible to be selected by any team in the following year's draft.

The 1976 agreement was approved by the courts.[26] This settlement agreement, reached through collective bargaining, had essentially the same effect on the players as it would have if it had been negotiated in the absence of litigation;[27] however, it was not enforced in the same way as a labor contract usually is. Negotiated agreements are interpreted and applied through the grievance procedure with arbitration available for impartial decision if necessary. In the *Robertson* settlement, the U.S. District Court retained jurisdiction to enforce the terms of the settlement by giving enforcement powers to a special master, whose decisions were subject to review by the court. Thus the judiciary became involved in what is normally carried out by the parties themselves through the grievance procedure and arbitration. The parties' choice of litigation rather than internal dispute resolution mechanisms is indicative of the poorly developed state of labor relations between the NBA and NBPA.

As might be expected, the complex and atypical arrangement for court review resulted in further litigation. This litigation arose over application of the old compensation rule, which the parties had agreed would remain in effect until the end of the 1980–81 season. Under this rule, when a free agent signed with a new team the two teams in question tried to reach agreement on compensation to the team that lost the player. If they were unable to agree, the commissioner was authorized to decide on compensation. The purpose of compensation was to make whole the old team rather than to punish the team that signs a free agent. Marvin Webster played out his option with the Seattle Supersonics and became a free agent for the 1978–79 season. He signed a five-year contract with the New York Knickerbockers for $600,000 a year. When Seattle and New York were unable to agree on compensation, Commissioner O'Brien took over and ruled that New York would have to give up to Seattle a player, Lonnie Shelton, as well as a first-round draft pick, and $450,000 cash. The special master, Columbia Law School professor Telford Taylor, reviewed this award. When the special master affirmed O'Brien's award, the matter was appealed to federal court by the NBPA. The union opposed O'Brien's award, because of the chilling effect it would have on the market for free agents.

The U.S. District Court found that the special master misinterpreted his authority and should have ruled that the commissioner's award was a penalty in violation of the agreement.[28] This decision was modified in part by the U.S. Court of Appeals, which held that the special master must set aside a compensation award by the commissioner if it is "substantially above" the value of the newly signed free agent so as to constitute a penalty.[29] After these decisions, the Webster compensation matter went back to Special Master Taylor, who overturned the commisioner's award. Later, Commissioner O'Brien modified his award to make it less punitive.

After the 1980–81 season, the compensation rule was eliminated. This left the teams with players who became free agents with only a right of first refusal for matching the player's contract offer from a new team. Since the right of first refusal remains in effect until the end of the 1986–87 season, the special master and federal courts continue to have a role in enforcing terms agreed to by the parties under the 1976 agreement. For example, in 1982 a dispute arose when Bernard King of the Golden State Warriors became a free agent and received an offer from the New York Knickerbockers for a five-year contract for $750,000 a year. Also included in the Knicks' "offer sheet" were a $620,000 signing bonus and a clause that would require a third team to pay King an additional $90,000 a year if the Warriors matched the offer and traded him to another club.[30] The Warriors objected to the signing bonus provision and the trade clause, and the matter went before Special Master Kingman Brewster, former president of Yale University, who upheld the Knicks' offer sheet. After further wrangling between the parties, the Warriors matched the offer, but then traded King to the Knicks for Michael Ray Richardson.

The lack of finality associated with the Brewster award and the early awards by Special Master Taylor illustrate the tenuous nature of enforcement decisions under the 1976 agreement. Although the special masters function like arbitrators, their decisions are not necessarily final or binding because the federal courts retain jurisdiction to review decisions. What are really matters of contract interpretation rather than law have been dragged into the courts where they do not belong. Nevertheless, the courts and special masters are properly involved under the settlement agreement reached by the parties themselves. Because it will be some time before the 1976 agreement resulting from the *Robertson* case finally expires, this unconventional, cumbersome, and expensive system of decision-making ping-pong will continue to hinder effective labor relations.

Franchise Movement

Decisions on franchise locations are vital to league interests. All professional team sports require approval for relocation of franchises. With the court decision in the Oakland Raiders move to Los Angeles, as discussed in chapter 3, the ability of leagues to prevent teams from moving is uncertain. The NBA's woes over this issue began in 1982 when Donald Sterling, owner of the San Diego Clippers, sought to move his team to Los Angeles because of operating losses. His unsuccessful attempt to secure permission resulted in a tangle of lawsuits and countersuits that caused the team to remain temporarily in San Diego. Then in 1984 Sterling, still without having obtained approval, moved the team to Los Angeles anyway. This prompted the NBA to initiate a $25 million suit against the Clippers, which sought to enforce the league's rights to approve franchise relocations. In 1984 the NBA changed the rule to require only a majority of owners for approval, but it is questionable whether the rule applies to the Clippers because approval was not sought for the most recent move before the rule modification. Pending determination of the NBA's suit against the Clippers, the club began play for the 1984–85 season in Los Angeles. It seems doubtful that it will be required to return to San Diego in light of the court decision in the Raiders case.

The old Kansas City Kings franchise began play in its new home of Sacramento in the 1985–86 season. This move was approved by the NBA, with the proviso that the team might be relocated unless Sacramento built a suitable arena by the 1987–88 season. At this writing, a new sixteen thousand–seat arena was under construction and its timely completion seemed likely.

1983 Agreement

In 1983, with losses averaging $700,000 per club, the players and owners worked out an agreement that is expected to eventually moderate NBA salaries. When negotiations for a new collective bargaining agreement began, the owners took the initiative. They hoped to get financial relief through a salary cap on each team. The owners' other principal demands were to reduce roster sizes from twelve to ten, eliminate first-class air travel, eliminate guaranteed player contracts, and establish a drug control program. The players showed little willingness to give up rights achieved under previous negotiated agreements. Their contract demands included a share in the percentage of future cable television revenues, guarantees on all contracts, and increases in pensions and severance pay.

Negotiations

Talks began in July 1982. The NBA's negotiating team was led by commissioner Larry O'Brien and his eventual successor David Stern, who was chief spokesman. Leading the union's bargaining group was general counsel Larry Fleisher, as chief negotiator, and NBPA president Bob Lanier of the Milwaukee Bucks. Stern and Fleisher had earlier confronted each other on numerous occasions at the bargaining table. Each had respect for the other, unlike the recent antagonists in baseball and football. When little was accomplished in the early bargaining sessions, the league filed a charge with the NLRB contending that the union had refused to negotiate over mandatory subjects of collective bargaining, particularly the salary moderation plan. It also threatened to put certain of its demands into effect if negotiations reached impasse.

After three months of negotiations, the parties reached tentative agreement on the concept that salary costs would be tied to team revenues, but no specific formula was developed. A gag rule was imposed on owners by the league, which indicated it would levy fines of up to $250,000 for making public statements about the negotiations. Strike talk was in the air, but it was not taken very seriously. Baseball and football had both recently suffered long strikes, and the NBA's financial situation was too precarious to allow it to become another victim. The opening of the regular season without incident was a reassuring sign that there would be no strike. Actually there was a strike, but it was by NBA referees who walked out for two months of the season, holding out for higher pay.[31]

In February 1983, all twenty-three player representatives voted that the deadline for reaching agreement was April 1. This date was chosen because the regular season ended on April 17, and pressure for settlement would build before the playoffs, which NBA owners count on heavily as a source of income. The focus in negotiations was the salary cap issue; the owners sought to place a $4 million limit on each team's payrolls, and teams with salaries above this limit would be prevented from signing free agents. As a quid pro quo, the owners offered to create a fund, in addition to salaries, that would share NBA revenues with the players. Although the players agreed in principle to a salary cap, they were uncertain as to how much it should be or when it should begin to take effect. The players indicated that if the negotiations were not completed by the deadline, a strike was one of the options they would consider. As a result of media pressure, strike talk began to escalate. Owner Sam Schulman stated publicly that he dared the players to strike.[32] Despite what would seem to be a clear violation of the NBA's gag rule on owners, there is no evidence that a fine was imposed for this statement. Perhaps irritated by the taunt, Fleisher announced shortly thereafter that the players would surely strike if the contract could not be reached on time.

As talks continued, the owner's proposal was revised to pay players' salaries based on 40 percent of the league's gross revenues. Given the fact that several individual players already had salaries close to what salary caps would allow for an entire team, it is not surprising that the NBPA did not accept the offer; however, there was an inducement for players to agree to some percentage of league revenues because of an anticipated bonanza from cable television in future years. The union's other principal objection to the salary cap scheme was that it might violate antitrust law and therefore should begin only after the 1986–87 season when the *Robertson* settlement expired. Moreover, the parties disagreed as to how much the salary cap would be. It was clear that the cap would affect clubs differently since the current NBA payrolls ranged from $1.1 million for the Indiana Pacers to $5 million for the Philadelphia 76ers.

About a week before the strike deadline, the owners raised their salary offer from 40 percent to 50 percent of league revenues over the next four years. The union countered with a demand of 53 percent. This narrowing in the parties' position renewed hopes for averting a strike.

On March 31, 1983, an agreement was reached between the parties in which the NBA came up to the NBPA's demand for a 53 percent guarantee of gross revenues. The salary cap provision was arranged to start with the 1984–85 season for most teams. Only the five teams with the highest payrolls—Los Angeles, New Jersey, New York, Philadelphia, and Seattle—were frozen at their current salary levels because they were already paying more than $3.6 million. The cap was scheduled to rise to $3.8 million in 1985–86, and to $4 million in 1986–87. These figures are a minimum cap, since the maximum cap is 53 percent of revenues. Only if the stated cap figures are less than 53 percent do they apply. For the 1985–86 season, the actual salary cap was set by the NBA at $4,233,000 per team.

The agreement is designed to provide greater parity between teams. Those in smaller markets, which offer salaries well below the cap, will be able to sign more outstanding players. Rich teams that have been active in the free agency market will still be able to sign outstanding players, but they will have to reduce their payrolls below the salary cap in order to make room for them. Each team can still match free agent offers made to their players by other clubs without affecting the salary cap.

The agreement is akin to profit-sharing plans in industry, but different in that the guarantees provided are so large. Also, if the cable television bonanza materializes, players will get the lion's share. Since the amounts available to players will rise with increases in gross revenue, they have an incentive to try to attract fans and spur interest in larger television contracts. On the other hand, players should not suffer much on the downside. There are

111

Basketball

minimum payrolls, determined by a complex formula, that should work out to about 90 percent of the salary ceiling.[33] Cash-poor teams will be helped to meet the minimum payroll by league subsidies. The players also won a guarantee of 253 jobs, only slightly fewer than the 276 jobs currently available. This would protect salaries in the event of a rash of bankruptcies in the NBA.

Salaries increased to $340,000 when the cap went into effect in 1984–85. The growth rate of salaries is expected to moderate unless there is a large increase in television revenues. The overall effect of the agreement should be to restrict the movement of star players and allow clubs a better opportunity to keep developing players who might otherwise take advantage of free agency.

Operation of the Salary Cap

The complexity of the salary cap provisions has resulted in confusion and uncertainty over club policies in signing players. The cap has generally limited the ability of rich teams to acquire free agents and restricted salaries of many first-year players, but there are loopholes that enable teams and players to evade the restrictions. These loopholes have to some extent undercut the purpose of the salary cap. For instance, teams are allowed to retain at any price one player who becomes a free agent, without his salary affecting the salary cap. This has enabled a team to sign another team's free agent, if it is below the salary cap, and then re-sign its own free agent regardless of the cost. Some teams have thus delayed signing their free agents until they have signed other free agents. In 1984, the Los Angeles Clippers traded Terry Cummings to the Milwaukee Bucks for three players with combined salaries of over $1.5 million. Two days after this trade, the Clippers signed their own free agent, Bill Walton, for about $1.4 million. The Clippers probably could not have made the trade under the salary cap if they had signed Walton first because they would have been over the salary cap. Another possible loophole is that players have been given sizable loans as part of their contractual arrangements. Since the collective bargaining agreement does not mention loans, there may be a way of compensating players without affecting the salary cap.

The salaries of first-year players have also caused controversy. The agreement provides that any team with a salary level at or over the salary cap can

112

sign a rookie to a one-year contract at the minimum salary of $75,000 for first-round picks ($65,000 for picks in later rounds of the draft). This has caused inequities for rookies. Akeem Olajuwon was signed by the Houston Rockets for an estimated $6.3 million over six years, and Michael Jordon by the Chicago Bulls for about $750,000 a year. Leon Wood and Charles Barkley, on the other hand, were signed by the Philadelphia 76ers for only $75,000 apiece, because that team was at the limit of the salary cap. Although a first-year player who signs a one-year contract at the minimum salary level has no restriction on how much he can be paid in subsequent years because later contracts do not count against the team's salary cap, some rookies are at a disadvantage compared to others. This inequity caused Leon Wood to file suit in federal district court challenging the salary cap on antitrust grounds, but the suit was dismissed by the court because the rules had been established by the owners and players' association in collective bargaining.

Apart from helping to reduce some rookie salaries, the salary cap has dampened free agency. Before the start of the 1984–85 season there were six unsigned free agents, including one so attractive as J. B. Carroll of the Golden State Warriors. In the past, free agents had little problem signing with new clubs, but the salary cap has limited the ability of clubs to pay the high salaries demanded by such players. Should this continue, it will help moderate salary levels since certain free agents will, in effect, be limited to offers from their current teams, with a consequent loss in bargaining power. Carroll, for example, left the United States to play professional basketball in Italy, but returned to the Warriors in 1985–86.

Aberrant Behavior

The NBA has an interest in presenting an image that reflects high morals and ethics. Because players are in the public eye, the league scrutinizes their actions both on and off the court to ensure proper behavior. Regulation has focused primarily on gambling, violence, and drugs.

Gambling

League officials have had two concerns about gambling. One is the problem of arrangements between players and gamblers to have players shave points to influence the outcome of games. It is not necessary that they throw the games by deliberately attempting to lose. All that is usually required is that players shave points by making mistakes or playing lethargically so that the final point spread beats the result anticipated by odds makers. It is difficult to determine the extent of such arrangements between players and gamblers because violators are rarely caught. Those cases that have come to light have been in the college ranks more than with professional leagues. Either the pros shave points less or are too clever to get caught.

The other gambling problem among players is direct betting on games. Player betting of any kind on the outcome of basketball games is prohibited by the NBA. Players who bet on the games they are not involved in are in a less reprehensible position than those who bet on their own games. The reason for this is that the presumption arises that a player has deliberately taken steps to influence the fate of his team so as to win bets.

In 1953 police of Fort Wayne, Indiana, conducted an investigation of the local NBA team known as the Pistons. As a result of the investigation, player Jack Molinas admitted making bets on Pistons' games with bookies on several occasions, but was not paid to throw games. The NBA constitution provided that players betting on the outcome of league games would be expelled by the league after due notice and hearing. League president Maurice Podoloff suspended Molinas indefinitely, without conducting a hearing. Molinas brought suit against the league to set aside the suspension and get back wages because no hearing had been held. The New York Supreme Court for New York County found that to hold a hearing would have been an empty gesture, since the player had already admitted gambling. Dismissing the complaint, the court further noted that to get relief in an equity court required "clean hands," and that the plaintiff's hands in this instance were not judged to be clean.[34] Molinas, who went to law school during his playing career, later became an attorney.

Other lawsuits have arisen when players have been denied admission to the NBA because of charges of gambling involvement during their college careers. One such player was Connie Hawkins, who was barred from the NBA for allegedly introducing a gambler to a fellow player and for association with gamblers in 1961 while at the University of Iowa. Hawkins sued the NBA for $6 million and in 1969 won a $1.5 million settlement. While the suit was in litigation Hawkins played for the Minnesota club in the ABA, and when the suit was settled he joined the Phoenix Suns of the NBA.

A similar court action was taken under the antitrust laws by a player who alleged that he was denied a chance to prove his eligibility for membership in the NBA.[35] Alphra Saunders played basketball at Bradley University between 1957 and 1961. He was not a regular starting player in his senior year and was expelled from school for failing to report receipt of money from men who tried to induce him to shave points in Bradley games. Saunders was not drafted by the NBA, and until 1969 when he filed suit he never communicated to any team that he had an interest in being an NBA player. The U.S. District Court found that the Clayton Act's four-year statute of limitations barred the suit because Saunders' alleged cause of action began in 1961 when he was not drafted by the NBA, but the suit was not filed until 1969. In any event, it seems doubtful that Saunders would have been able to collect damages from the NBA because he was not a player likely to have been drafted by the NBA even if he had not had the gambling incident.

In 1982 the NBA became the first professional sports league to introduce an education program to make players aware of the threats of bribery in sports and implications of wagering on sports contests. Presentations are made by specially trained FBI agents and former players. This education program also includes instruction on drug abuse.

Violence

Fighting by players has long been a problem in the NBA. What makes the problem so acute is that players wear hardly any protective gear to insulate them from physical violence. The most publicized fighting incident in the NBA occurred in 1977 in a game between the Los Angeles Lakers and Houston Rockets. When Kermit Washington of the Lakers began to fight with Kevin Kunnert of the Rockets, Kunnert's teammate Rudy Tomjanovich ran to try to mediate the confrontation. Washington hit Tomjanovich a terrible blow in the face, causing fractures of the face and skull, a broken nose, a separated upper jaw, and a cerebral concussion.[36] Washington was fined $10,000 by Commissioner O'Brien and suspended from further play. He was later reinstated but lost a total of $60,000 from the fine and forfeited salary.

Tomjanovich sued the Lakers, and a jury in the Southern District of Texas awarded him $3.2 million in damages. However, the case was later settled, with Tomjanovich getting about a half million dollars.[37] That the Lakers knew of Washington's reputation as a fighter and should have been able to prevent the incident weighed against their escaping liability. Tomjanovich suffered permanent injury, but later returned to play in the NBA.

A few months after the Tomjanovich incident, NBA owners gave Commissioner O'Brien sweeping powers to levy fines and suspend players in order to curb violence during games. A fine of up to $10,000 was authorized even if the fighting player was not ejected from the game. Several players have been fined for fighting since then, usually for $1,500, and fighting in the NBA, which had become almost epidemic in 1977, has been reduced in recent years. Another step taken by the league was to establish a joint committee on violence with the NBPA. But after about a year of meetings, the player representatives on the committee withdrew because of a disagreement over the NBPA's proposal for a third referee to try to limit violence and provide better-officiated games. The owners' representatives viewed this addition as too expensive to implement.

Drugs

Drug abuse by NBA players began to surface in 1980. Various reports indicated that anywhere from 40 to 75 percent of the players were using cocaine. Before this time, for about ten years, the NBA hired a medical consultant and team doctors to regularly inform players about the evils of drug abuse. But the problem was not widespread then, except for the use of pep pills to get up for games. In 1980 the NBA created a Drug Education and Prevention Committee, including owners, coaches, trainers, and team doctors—but no players, to increase drug education programs. A twenty-four-hour counseling service was established in 1981 by the NBA and NBPA. Counselors from the Life Extension Institute, which has clinics in New York, Baltimore, Los Angeles, and Minneapolis, were made available to players or members of their families for a variety of problems, including drugs. Participation in this program is confidential, with no disclosure to team or league.

In the 1982–83 collective bargaining the NBA proposed urinalysis for all players. But the players rejected drug testing, and the issue was dropped from negotiations. After agreement was reached on other issues, the parties began to reconsider the need for an elaborate drug control program that included testing. In September 1983, these negotiations produced the most extensive program yet developed in professional sports. Agreement was reached because the players decided to act as a moving force in bringing it about. They had earlier won a 53 percent share of all revenues in the league and reasoned that a strong program would improve their media and fan image. Higher revenues from television and attendance would increase the players' monetary rewards.

The basic program is simple and tough. A player who comes forth voluntarily with a drug (cocaine or heroin) problem is provided treatment with no penalty. If a player comes forth a second time he receives treatment, but his pay is suspended. If this occurs a third time, the player is banned from the game. Three strikes and out. A player who does not come forth voluntarily and gets caught using drugs is immediately banned from further play. Players who are asked to take a drug test and refuse are also banned. So are players involved in the distribution of drugs, without actually using them. Players who are banished can apply for reinstatement after two years. If they are clean then, reinstatement is likely.

An independent expert on drug detection was hired by the league to authorize drug testing for players believed by the NBA or NBPA to be using drugs, based on information given to the NBA or NBPA. This expert can order tests on a player four times during a six-week period, without notice to the player. Instead of requesting testing, the league or players' association can seek a hearing on the player's alleged use of drugs before an impartial arbitrator. If the arbitrator determines that the player has used drugs illegally, the player is expelled from the league.

Shortly after the program was announced, a few players came forward for treatment. An amnesty period was established until December 31, 1983, so that no players would be suspended until after this time. The program was expanded by the NBA board of governors to include owners, general managers, coaches, trainers, and all league employees. The first incident under the new procedure occurred when the New Jersey Nets placed player Michael Ray Richardson on waivers after he refused drug treatment. Richardson had been twice previously treated for cocaine abuse. He filed a grievance to gain reinstatement with the club and entered a drug treatment center for a third time. Richardson was reinstated, but agreed to forfeit pay for games missed, drop his grievance, and take drug tests. Complicating the Richardson matter was the fact that he was waived and reinstated by the Nets during the amnesty period.

In the 1984–85 season, two players who were released by their clubs were found in drug tests to have used cocaine. John Drew of the Utah Jazz and John Lucas of the Houston Rockets were both second-time offenders under the NBA's program. In 1986 Michael Ray Richardson became a third-time offender and thus the first player to be banned under the drug program.

The NBA's drug control program has been criticized as being too punitive. Some observers feel that threat of punishment will not deter drug abuse. The program, however, is far harder on players who get caught without voluntarily disclosing their problems. It encourages players to acknowledge their illness and obtain treatment. Their pay even continues during the first treatment period. No drug control program is going to work perfectly, but the NBA's approach appears to be the kind of program that should serve as a model for other professional team sports.

5. Hockey

The sport of ice hockey is relatively unfamiliar to persons living in the temperate zones of the United States. Yet it has a wide following in the northern part of the country and is an extremely popular sport in Canada, the European nations, and the Soviet Union. The game provides a combination between the sports of soccer and field hockey, with six players on each side.

Hockey's origins are somewhat obscure, but the game, roughly as we know it today, appears to have evolved in Canada in the last half of the nineteenth century. Early rules were laid down by students at Montreal's McGill University in 1875. At that time, organized hockey was played exclusively at the amateur level, and the first national hockey association was formed in 1885 with teams from Montreal, Quebec, and Ottawa.[1] In 1893 the governor general of Canada, Lord Stanley, donated a cup to be presented to the Canadian amateur hockey champions.

Professional hockey became prominent in 1909 when the National Hockey Association (NHA) was organized for teams in eastern Canada; and in 1911 when the Pacific Coast Hockey League was formed among teams in western Canada and the United States. When these two leagues held a championship playoff in 1912, the Stanley Cup presented to the victor became the symbol of professional, rather than amateur, supremacy. When the NHA disbanded in 1917, the National Hockey League (NHL) was formed and today remains

119

the sport's major league. By 1942 the NHL included six teams: Boston, Chicago, Detroit, Montreal, New York Rangers, and Toronto. In 1967 the league expanded to twelve teams, and in 1974 to eighteen teams. This expansion was followed by several franchise shifts and realignments, such as the addition of teams from the rival World Hockey Association (WHA) in 1979, so that the NHL in 1986 had twenty-one teams in the United States and Canada.

Major league hockey is the least economically important of the four sports comprising the professional sports industry today. This is in large part due to its lack of a network television contract for the United States and the limited seating capacities of arenas. The numerous industrial relations issues in hockey, some similar to those of other sports and some unique, make for interesting examination. Of all the sports, hockey has a larger measure of cooperation between management and the players' union. Collective bargaining has not been characterized by the acrimony that is common in other sectors of the sports industry.

Economics of Hockey

The overall financial state of the NHL in recent years has not been healthy. Hockey is played in relatively small arenas, with typical seating capacities of about fifteen thousand, and many teams find it difficult to cover payroll, travel, lease, and equipment costs. Without a network television contract, NHL teams do not derive the significant revenues from that source that other major professional team sports do. In 1984–85, about a third of the teams in the NHL were profitable, a third were breaking even, and a third were losing money. Since World War II, only one team has gone bankrupt, the Pittsburgh Penguins in 1975, but if losses continue to mount for weaker teams in the league, some could go under.

Attendance

Because television revenues are not so bountiful in hockey as in other sports, the success of individual clubs is closely linked to gate receipts. Although seating capacities are limited, each team plays an eighty-game regular season, and there are numerous playoff games for many clubs. Revenue from attendance in the NHL was about $135 million in 1983–84, which con-

Table 5.1   NHL Attendance, 1975–85

Year	Total Games	Total Attendance	Average Attendance
1975–76	720	9,103,761	12,644
1976–77	720	8,563,890	11,894
1977–78	720	8,526,564	11,842
1978–79	680	8,333,609	12,255
1979–80	840	10,533,623	12,540
1980–81	840	10,725,134	12,768
1981–82	840	10,710,894	12,751
1982–83	840	11,020,610	13,120
1983–84	840	11,359,386	13,523
1984–85	840	12,307,913	14,640

Source: National Hockey League.

stituted about 75 percent of total revenue.[2] Attendance at NHL games for the past decade is shown in table 5.1. Apart from the decline that began in the mid-1970s and continued for several years, attendance has grown steadily, if unspectacularly, in the recent past.

There appears to be a negative correlation between the extent of violence at NHL games and attendance levels. While some fans react favorably to player fighting, most are turned off by violence because it detracts from the artistry of the game. Hockey was meant to be played by swift skaters, deft passers, and hard shooters, not by goons and muggers. When played cleanly, hockey is a wonderfully exciting sport for live viewing. The skills of great players like Wayne Gretsky of the Edmonton Oilers and Mike Bossy of the New York Islanders require unspoiled play to develop to their fullest extent, and the NHL's efforts at curbing violence have succeeded in attracting more fans to arenas. The players themselves have control over their salary potential by curbing excessive violence to attract spectator interest.

Television

From 1956 to 1975 two major American television networks, CBS and NBC, had an on-again, off-again contractual arrangement with the NHL for presenting games. Since 1975, however, the networks have disdained the NHL because of poor ratings in previous years. Despite the lack of immediate prospects for an American network contract, the NHL seems to be on the threshold of a significant expansion in television revenues from cable. Like the NBA, the NHL is largely pursuing a strategy of catering to local markets rather than a large national audience. Local and network cable and pay television agreements direct hockey to the attention of viewers who have a keener interest in the sport. Through narrower television marketing the revenue base for the league can be increased because it is more profitable for the television industry to present selective packages to viewers. It is therefore expected that a growing share of NHL revenues will be derived from television. Although it is doubtful that this source will produce income of the same magnitude as it does in football and baseball, it could become just as large a proportion of the smaller scale revenues of the NHL.

Several signs of this revenue potential are already emerging. In 1985, the NHL signed a three-year agreement for $20 million with the ESPN cable network for exclusive rights to televise thirty-three regular season games, the all-star game, and all the Stanley Cup playoffs. These games are presented nationwide in the United States, but not in Canada. The Canadian counterpart to ESPN is the Canadian Sports Network. Also, two games a week are presented in a show called "Hockey Night in Canada" by the Canadian Broadcasting Company. These games receive exceptionally high ratings. The real market growth potential, however, is in televising games in regions where the games of local teams can be shown to a loyal group of followers. Several NHL teams already present games on local pay or free television. In the United States, these games are mostly shown under cable arrangements. The most lucrative of the league's local television contracts in 1983–84 was the Philadelphia Flyers' $5 million annual deal.[3] Altogether, the NHL's television revenues approximately trebled from 1978 to 1984. But the estimated $35 million in revenues in the latter year was still quite small compared with that for other sports' television arrangements. It appears likely that in the future more games will be shown locally under cable contracts and that selected games from the Stanley Cup playoffs, especially the final series, will be televised by a major American network. Another possible direction for the industry is for more NHL owners to seek packaged sports arrangements on local cable television. Because of their overlapping seasons, a logical package is hockey and basketball. Jerry Buss, who owns both the Kings (NHL) and Lakers (NBA) has already established such a precedent in Los Angeles by combining these sports into a single fee television package, a good example of horizontal integration in marketing. Another example is provided by Ed Snider, owner of the Philadelphia Flyers and the Spectrum, a hockey and basketball arena. He has tied together his ownership interests with a television company, Prism, that broadcasts sports over local cable television. With the growth of television exposure and concomitant increases in revenues, a lively debate is likely to occur over the distribution of these revenues among teams.

Salaries

In the absence of a significant increase in television revenues, hockey is unable to support the increases in player salaries that have occurred in other sports. The highest paid NHL players by position are goaltenders, followed by defensemen, and then forwards.[4] Table 5.2 shows the average salaries in the NHL for selected years since 1972. The rapid increase in the 1970s was largely due to the competition over player salaries caused by the World Hockey Association. Since the demise of the WHA in 1979, salaries have increased at a more modest pace.

The contracts signed by the number-one draft choice in hockey are another indication of salary trends. Like their counterparts in the NFL and NBA, these players go directly from the amateur ranks to the major leagues, but the top draft choices are similar to those in baseball in that they are usually signed at a younger average age. Top draft choices in baseball do not

Table 5.2   Average Salaries in the NHL

1972	1975	1977	1979	1981	1983	1985
$44,109	$74,000	$96,000	$101,000	$110,000	$125,000	$140,000

Source: Data for 1972–77 from Ray Kennedy and Nancy Williamson, "Money: The Monster Threatening Sports," *Sports Illustrated*, 17 July 1978, 46. Later years estimated by the author from data from NHL and NHLPA.

Table 5.3   Salaries of Number-One Draft Choices in the NHL, 1975–85

Year	Player	Team	Annual Salary Plus Bonus
1975	Mel Bridgman	Philadelphia	$100,000 + $100,000
1976	Rick Green	Washington	125,000 + 150,000
1977	Dale McCourt	Detroit	100,000 + 100,000
1978	Bobby Smith	Minnesota	125,000 + 150,000
1979	Rob Ramage	Colorado*	110,000 + 125,000
1980	Doug Wickenheiser	Montreal	80,000 + 70,000
1981	Dale Hawerchuck	Winnipeg	200,000 + 100,000
1982	Gord Kluzak	Boston	80,000 + 100,000
1983	Brian Lawton	Minnesota	100,000 + 125,000
1984	Mario Lemieux	Pittsburgh	300,000 + 150,000
1985	Wendel Clark	Toronto	100,000 + 175,000

Source: Data for 1975–83 from *Sporting News*, 7 July 1984, 47; data for 1984 from "Pittsburgh Lands a Rare Bird," *Sports Illustrated*, 15 October 1984, 57; and 1985 from *Sporting News*, 9 September 1985, 48.
Note: *The Colorado Rockies franchise was transferred to New Jersey for the 1982–83 season.

---

typically go directly to the major leagues since they require seasoning in the minors. Compared with the salaries of football and basketball number-one draft choices in recent years, hockey players are getting only about one-third to one-half as much pay (table 5.3).

Pensions

The NHL's pension plan was initiated in 1947 with the approval of the players. They agreed to contribute $900 a year from individual salaries, and the league agreed to contribute two-thirds of the proceeds from the annual all-star game plus 25 percent of the ticket sales from playoff games. Eligibility for benefits was established at age forty-five. For the 1985–86 season, the age for eligibility remained at forty-five, but the pension plan no longer required direct out-of-pocket contributions by the players.[5] They receive $1,000 (Canadian dollars) annually for each full year of credited service (seventy games), and credit can be received by a player even though he may be temporarily assigned to a minor league club. Half the funding for pensions is provided by the NHL; and half is an obligation of the NHLPA, which is expected to fund its share out of proceeds from "international" hockey games, the annual Canada Cup matches involving amateur and NHL players from countries such as Canada, the United States, Sweden, Czechoslovakia, the Soviet Union, and Finland. If a player is forced to retire prematurely because of an injury, he is awarded a pension credit for each year of disability until ten years of pension credit have accrued.

This pension plan has good potential for future growth in contributions and benefits from the increased interest in international competition. Although hockey is not as important from an overall economic standpoint as other professional team sports, its pension plan is relatively generous. A sound pension fund is crucial to hockey because most players are very young and relatively uneducated when they begin serious competition in preparation for the professional ranks. Many are unable to derive significant incomes from talents apart from their playing skills and professional reputations. Unlike other professional athletes, who are, on the whole, better educated from their college days, hockey players' potential for postretirement income is thus more constricted.

Structure of Employment

Government

The overall influence of government on industrial relations in hockey has not been as significant as in other sports. This is ironic, since the governments of two countries—Canada and the United States—might become involved through the actions of legislatures, courts, and administrative agencies. Perhaps because of the distinctive, international setting for hockey, neither government seems inclined to intrude on developments in the sport. A more likely reason for the relative noninvolvement is that labor and management have not looked to government as a source of dispute resolution so much as in other sports. The parties have chosen to work out their problems at the bargaining table and through informal discussions, more often than they resort to outside assistance. This is not to say that government action has been totally absent from hockey, only that labor and management have not typically felt a need to rely on this source.

The American courts were active in helping NHL players jump leagues to play with teams in the World Hockey Association. Nevertheless, government's role in such intraleague matters as free agency, draft rules, collective bargaining conduct, and drug abuse has been limited. In Canada, Parliament has threatened to take a strong position on violence in hockey, but leaders within the sport have succeeded in heading off regulation by trying to clean up their own house.

Apart from the traditional areas of government influence on sports, which will be addressed in detail later in the chapter, two interesting applications of government participation have affected the industry. One involves the divergent application of tax laws and currency exchange between Canada and the United States. Canada's tax structure imposes a heavy burden on clubs and players operating in that country. Incomes are taxed at higher rates, and depreciation of players is not allowed. There are also differences stemming from the disparity in value of the Canadian and American dollars, with the latter worth about 20 percent more in recent years. Canadian teams pay their players in Canadian dollars. Although most of the players in the NHL are Canadian citizens, most of the clubs are situated in the United States. When Canadian athletes play for American teams, they are paid in U.S. currency and gain a substantial advantage on the dollar exchange. Other things being equal, a given player would be more inclined to play for an American rather than a Canadian team.

Determining amateur status for purposes of competing in the Olympic games is a second, important area of government involvement that potentially affects all major professional team sports. In many cases, the rules for determining amateur status are left up to the appropriate sports governing bodies. Eligibility rules are stricter in some sports than in others, which causes inconsistencies and inequities. Hockey is governed by the rules of the International Olympic Committee (IOC), but the International Ice Hockey Federation and Olympic committees in the individual countries also influence individual player participation. At the time of the 1984 Winter Olympics in Sarajevo, Yugoslavia, the IOC had not approved the rules for participation set down by the international hockey federation. There was, however, unanimous agreement among participating countries that any player not currently under a professional contract would be eligible to compete in the games. A dispute arose when the Canadians tried to use players who were under professional contract. They interpreted the rules to allow this if an athlete had played in fewer than ten NHL games. Their attempt caused a protest to be filed by the United States, which led to heated recriminations between representatives of the two countries. R. Alan Eagleson, a Canadian and executive director of the NHL players' union, objected that certain members of the 1980 United States team had been ineligible to play in Lake Placid. Those players, however, had offers outstanding from NHL clubs that had not yet been accepted, which is different from being under contract and having actually played in NHL games. The dispute was resolved when the IOC ruled that five players—two Canadians, two Italians, and one Austrian—were ineligible for competition at Sarajevo.

This incident points up the difficulty of determining eligibility and the irregular line between amateur and professional status in different sports. Athletes from many competing nations in various Olympic sports are subsidized generously by the state or corporations. The day may not be far off when this sham amateurism is dropped and the Olympics are in whole or part thrown open to competition between all athletes, whether "amateur" or professional. There is a good chance, for instance, that regular NHL players will be declared eligible to compete in the 1988 winter games in Calgary.

Management

Outspoken owners who meddle with the performance of their teams on the field have always existed in sports. They are probably more conspicuous today because of the high risk of operating teams with rapidly escalating payrolls. Hockey owners have been relatively aloof in the past, but a new breed of owners—flamboyant entrepreneurs and large corporations—is taking a more businesslike approach to running the franchises, which often includes entertainment hype to stir interest among fans and the media. Players are more openly criticized, coaches are fired more often, and team strategy is dictated from the front office—all in the interest of keeping the club in the headlines. The owners reason that since they pay the bills, they have the right to operate the team as they see fit. Sports ownership has never been a totally benign business, but modern owners are far more cutthroat and egoistic. They figure they have to be tougher because competition is keener.

Table 5.4 shows the ownership of teams in the NHL. In general, teams do not change hands as often as teams in other sports. Like their counterparts in other sports, the new owners are more apt to be individuals or corporations

Hockey

Table 5.4 Ownership of NHL Franchises

Team	Division	Principal Owner	Other Interests
Boston Bruins	Adams	Group headed by James Brennan and Godfrey Wood	Investments, real estate
Buffalo Sabres	Adams	Knox brothers	Real estate, insurance
Calgary Flames	Smythe	Six individuals	Oil, real estate
Chicago Black Hawks	Norris	William Wirtz	Diversified interests
Detroit Red Wings	Norris	Michael Ilitch	Pizza parlors
Edmonton Oilers	Smythe	Peter Pocklington	Meatpacking, real estate
Hartford Whalers	Adams	Aetna Life & Casualty	Insurance
Los Angeles Kings	Smythe	Jerry Buss	L.A. Lakers (NBA), L.A. Forum (arena), real estate
Minnesota North Stars	Norris	Gund brothers	Cleveland Coliseum, real estate, insurance, Cleveland Cavaliers (NBA)
Montreal Canadiens	Adams	Molson Breweries	Beer
New Jersey Devils	Patrick	John McMullen	Shipbuilding
New York Islanders	Patrick	John D. Pickett	Diversified interests
New York Rangers	Patrick	Madison Square Garden Corp. (Gulf & Western)	Conglomerate businesses
Philadelphia Flyers	Patrick	Ed Snider	Philadelphia Spectrum (arena), insurance
Pittsburgh Penguins	Patrick	Edward DeBartolo	San Francisco 49ers (NFL), Pittsburgh Civic Arena, shopping centers
Quebec Nordiques	Adams	Carling O'Keefe Brewery	Beer
St. Louis Blues	Norris	Harry Ornest	Real estate
Toronto Maple Leafs	Norris	Harold Ballard	Maple Leaf Gardens (arena), Hamilton Tiger-Cats (CFL)
Vancouver Canucks	Smythe	Frank Griffiths family	British Columbia Television
Washington Capitals	Patrick	Abe Pollin	Capital Centre (arena), Washington Bullets (NBA)
Winnipeg Jets	Smythe	Barry Shenkarow	Real estate

Source: Compiled from data furnished by the NHL, and various published sources.

with interests that relate to the entertainment industry and to businesses that derive significant portions of their incomes from sports. Also, a large share of the owners in the NHL have made substantial monies in real estate transactions. Some own sports arenas and teams in other professional leagues. Many are self-made men, throwbacks to the early captains of industry in America and Canada. Two of the teams are owned by breweries, Montreal by Molson and Quebec by Carling O'Keefe.

Despite an increase in public visibility as individuals, hockey owners as a group hold together more on league policy issues than is the general rule. Each owner has representation on the NHL's board of governors, which, along with the league president, determines overall policies. Intraorganizational league strength is in part due to the relative stability of leadership as vested in the office of the NHL president. The league does not have a commissioner as do baseball, football, and basketball. Enlightened leadership in the office of the president was demonstrated by Clarence Campbell, who headed the league from 1946 to 1977. A former Rhodes scholar, NHL referee (1929–40), and prosecutor at the Nuremberg trials, Campbell oversaw league expansion from six to eighteen teams during his presidency. This kindly but tough Scot was succeeded as NHL president by John A. Ziegler, Jr., the first American to serve in this position. A lawyer, who graduated from the University of Michigan, Ziegler was formerly an executive with the Detroit Red Wings and served as chair of the NHL board of governors. Ziegler has demonstrated able leadership, but like Campbell, has experienced difficulty in controlling player violence in the NHL. His forte appears to be excellent understanding of labor relations issues and an evenhanded approach to negotiations with the players' union.

Teams in the NHL have farm arrangements with clubs in the Junior A amateur leagues of Canada (the Ontario Hockey League and Quebec Hockey League),[6] as well as with professional teams in the American Hockey League and Western Hockey League. The Central Hockey League, previously a minor league feeder system for NHL teams, suspended operations in the 1984–85 season. Like other major professional team sports, hockey drafts amateur players through a system based on an inverse relationship of final team standings. This is done to achieve parity, but some of the less successful teams have traded away top amateur draft choices for veteran players, which has not usually proved to be a wise strategy.

Labor

At one time nearly all the players in the NHL were from Canada. In recent years this has changed in two important ways. One is the influx of Americans into the league. This is the result of better coaching of U.S. youngsters, increased participation in youth leagues, and improved college programs at schools like Minnesota, Wisconsin, North Dakota, Cornell, Boston College, and Providence. The other is the increased signing of players from the burgeoning amateur and professional ranks in Europe. In the 1985–86 season, for example, about 76 percent of the 508 players on NHL rosters were from Canada, nearly all of whom were drafted from the Junior A leagues. But U.S. born players constituted 12 percent, most of them from Minnesota, Massachusetts, Michigan, and New York. The rest of the players were from other countries, mostly Sweden, Czechoslovakia, and Finland.[7] In 1983–84, the number one pick in the amateur draft was for the first time an American, Brian Lawton from Providence, Rhode Island, who was selected by the Minnesota North Stars. Until recently, the Montreal Canadiens, the most successful dynasty in hockey over the years, never recruited from American high schools and colleges, but the Canadiens' 1984–85 roster included six Americans. The average age of players in the NHL is 25.4, and careers there last an average of 4.8 years. Professional hockey players are relatively young because they are eligible to be drafted if they reach at least eighteen years of age by January 1 of the following season.

In 1957 league players established a union, the National Hockey League Players Association (NHLPA), with Ted Lindsay of the Detroit Red Wings as president. The players organized to fill a perceived power vacuum in their relations with management, as well as to provide a means of helping promote the popularity of the sport. The players were generally contented, receiving a minimum salary of $6,500, which was $500 more than that for baseball players. A generous player pension plan had been established a decade earlier. It was not long, however, before the union sought to flex its muscle through its legal counsel, J. Norman Lewis, who also represented major league baseball players. The hockey players were miffed over a 1956 television contract with CBS that provided no share for them. Lewis therefore threatened an antitrust suit against the league, but the dispute was resolved when the owners agreed to contribute monies from television to enhance player pensions.

Other than this confrontation, NHL players did not accomplish much through their union in the next decade or so. Then in 1967 Alan Eagleson, a Toronto lawyer and players' agent in salary negotiations with owners, became head of the reconstituted NHLPA. Eagleson quickly grasped the reins of power and achieved formal recognition of the union by the league. His influence over the years has been remarkable. Not only did he help the players attain unimagined salaries, but he took a large measure of control over international hockey, bringing it from a game dominated by amateur play to multimillion dollar professional competition in the annual six-nation Canada Cup. Today Eagleson wears many hats. He heads the union, to which virtually all players now belong; is chief negotiator for Hockey Canada, the non-profit corporation that administers Canada's involvement in international events; and represents about 10 percent of the NHL players in their salary negotiations with owners. Many observers perceive Eagleson as by far the most powerful individual force in hockey.

Although Eagleson has many admirers, especially among the players, owners, and international hockey officials, he also has numerous critics. Some have charged that he takes too soft a line in collective bargaining. Detractors point to the fact that hockey salaries have not risen as sharply as in other sports, and that the free agency system in hockey does not work to the advantage of the players. They also cite the potential conflict of interest that arises in that he represents players as a whole, some individual players, and management itself when he negotiates international agreements that bring revenues to owners.

One of Eagleson's most prominent clients, Bobby Orr, a famous defenseman, charged that Eagleson mishandled his financial affairs. In 1976, when Orr became a free agent, he left the Boston Bruins and signed with the Chicago Black Hawks for $3 million over five years. But Orr's damaged knees did not hold up so he retired in 1978. Orr charged that his Chicago deal, which Eagleson negotiated, guaranteed him $1.5 million, but only after lengthy litigation was he able to collect less than $1 million.

Supporters of Eagleson counter that he has not pushed owners to the wall because of the precarious financial straits of several teams in the NHL. They see no obvious conflict of interest in his serving as an agent for individual players. As for representing management in international transactions, supporters note that much of the revenue from these deals goes to the players' pension fund. It seems clear that Eagleson's sagacity has helped keep the league together while at the same time making a lot of money for all concerned, including himself.

Negotiation and Agreements

Hockey has an unusual system of collective bargaining in that negotiation is more apt to be undertaken spontaneously in response to newly emerging issues. Reopening of contractual provisions is not uncommon in American and Canadian industries as a whole, but subsequent negotiations during the life of a contract are usually limited to a specified issue, such as wages. The "evergreen" concept, under which existing contracts are changed or added to in material part, was particularly common in early negotiations in hockey. From 1967, when the NHLPA was formally recognized, until 1975, understandings reached in annual negotiations were recorded in formal minutes that collectively formed the parties' contractual arrangement. In 1975 and 1982, five-year conventional agreements were negotiated, but these agreements have also been subject to frequent modification. Responsibility for collective bargaining is vested in the Owner-Player Council, which meets in February and June each year to review contractual arrangements. Continuous bargaining has the advantage of adapting to dynamic conditions affecting the sport. Although the likelihood of disputes, and perhaps strikes, would seem to be increased by this practice, the trust and respect that the parties share in hockey have made for relatively smooth revision.

Salary and Grievance Arbitration

Salary arbitration was initiated in 1969. The method of arbitration has evolved over the years from the use of two arbitrators, who if unable to reach agreement would be supplemented by a third arbitrator who would decide, to the current practice of having a single permanent umpire arbitrate disputes. The jurisdiction of arbitration, however, has always been limited to salary disputes that arise during the option year in the standard players' contract. This application of arbitration is similar to the practice in baseball; that is, for players not eligible for free agency who wish to sign a new contract with their existing club but are unable to agree on salary terms, either the player or club can instigate arbitration to resolve the dispute. Unlike arbitration in baseball, which uses a variety of arbitrators to resolve disputes, the hockey umpire, Gary E. Schreider, is not limited to choice from the final offers of the participants. Criteria established in the collective bargaining agreement for making the arbitration decision are similar to those set forth under the baseball agreement, and they include such factors as overall performance by the player, physical defects, length of service, and special qualities of leadership.

Neither the NHL nor the NHLPA release data on salary arbitrations, so it is unknown whether players have used this procedure effectively to achieve significant increases. In the last ten years only about 2 percent of the players have utilized salary arbitration annually, so salaries reached in arbitration are apparently not much different from those arrived at through negotiations, and although there is little incentive for players to go to arbitration, there is no indication that hockey's salary arbitration procedure is not working to the satisfaction of all concerned parties. That the percentage of baseball players utilizing salary arbitration is somewhat higher seems due to the more paternalistic relationship that exists between players and owners in hockey.

Following the precedent in other sports, final decisions on grievances resulting from the interpretation or application of negotiated agreements in hockey were initially in the hands of the league president. If the parties were unable to resolve grievances, management had the last word. This practice was changed in hockey through collective bargaining in 1975, and the revised grievance procedure remains operative. Grievances over the interpretation or application of the negotiated agreement, club rules, and propriety of discipline are subject to arbitration. Enforcement of contracts through grievance arbitration is as protective of union interests as in any sport. But as in other sports, the league president in hockey (or the commissioners in other sports) retains some control on matters of discipline. The president continues to have the final word on issues concerning the severity of discipline meted out to players. Thus, whether a player should have been disciplined in the first place—say, for game violence—is subject to grievance and arbitration, but the reasonableness of the fine or suspension given the player is for the president to determine. The president also retains final jurisdiction for disputes stemming from the interpretation or application of provisions in the standard players' contract negotiated individually between the player and club.

Free Agency

Hockey players were not allowed to become free agents before the World Hockey Association began play in 1972. Legal challenges to NHL control of players resulted in several players moving to teams in the WHA by achieving free agency status. As a result of the law cases, the NHL unilaterally adopted a policy of seeking to retain players for only one year beyond the expiration of their standard players' contracts. In 1975 this policy was incorporated into the NHL's negotiated agreement with the NHLPA. Under this agreement, a system for compensating clubs that lost free agents was established. Known as "equalization," the club that signed a free agent was required to reach agreement with the player's former team. If the clubs were unable to agree on compensation, the dispute was submitted to final-offer arbitration, under which the arbitrator selects one of the parties' positions without amendment.

The equalization system did not work to the advantage of players. Clubs were reluctant to sign free agents because of the uncertainty of penalties imposed through compensation. Hockey's system was not as onerous as the old Rozelle Rule in football, because final compensation decisions were assigned to an arbitrator rather than the top league official. Until 1982 when the procedure was changed, just three arbitration cases on equalization were decided. In the most celebrated of these cases, Rogatien Vachon, goaltender for the Los Angeles Kings, became a free agent and signed with the Detroit Red Wings. As compensation, the arbitrator ruled that the Red Wings would have to give up its leading scorer, a young forward named Dale McCourt. This led to McCourt's filing suit to challenge the arbitration procedure on antitrust grounds. The federal court of appeals denied relief to the player, holding that the equalization procedure and subsequent decision of the arbitrator were valid.[8] The court's rationales were that the equalization procedure had been arrived at through collective bargaining between the NHL and NHLPA; and the decision to award McCourt to the Kings as compensation for the loss of free-agent Vachon was made by a neutral arbitrator rather than a league president or commissioner.

In the face of the *McCourt* decision and the inability of players to achieve economic gains through free agency, the NHLPA sought to alter the system of equalization in its favor. During several months of bargaining in 1981–82, the parties remained far apart on the issue. Although the players began talking about a possible strike to enhance their position in negotiations, at no point was a strike imminent because neither side wanted one and each believed that compromise could be worked out. In August 1982 agreement was finally reached.

The centerpiece of the modified equalization system is a procedure for determining free agency compensation based on the salary of the player involved. No compensation is required if the player makes under $85,000. For players with salaries above that amount, a graduated scale allows choices in the amateur draft or players from the roster of the team that signs the free agent:

$85,000–99,000: third-round choice.

$100,000–124,999: second and third-round choice.

$125,000–149,999: first-round choice *or* player from new club, with new club having protected eight players, including player signed.

$150,000–199,999: first and second-round choices *or* player from new club with six players protected, including player signed.

$200,000 and over: two first-round choices *or* player from new club with four players protected, including player signed.

A right of first refusal was also established to allow an existing club to retain a free agent by matching the offer of a new team. Free-agent players thirty-three years of age or over can change teams without compensation required. If a free agent is under age twenty-four or has less than five years professional experience, the old system of equalization applies, with clubs submitting to final-offer arbitration if they are unable to agree on compensation.

The 1982 agreement, designed to liberalize free agency, has had a mixed effect, but one that appears to reflect the interests of the principals. If free agency were wide open, the clubs in Canada would probably survive because of high attendance, revenues from cable television, and domestic beer sponsorship. But some U.S. teams would fold, and the vitality of the league would be sapped. Salaries of top players would escalate rapidly, but many jobs would be lost by average players. This scenario is not desirable to anyone, and thus limitation must be placed on free agency.

Judging from the numbers of players who have become free agents under the new agreement, one might conclude that a great deal of liberalization has occurred. Before the 1983–84 and 1984–85 seasons, for example, about

180 free agents were available for signing by new clubs.[9] These figures, however, are misleading for three reasons. Many of these players were given termination contracts by their teams that force them to become free agents, and, of the total free agents, only about 15 percent (twenty to twenty-five players a year) had salaries that were high enough to justify equalization payments if they were signed by other clubs. Perhaps most important, most of the free agents subject to equalization were players in the lower range of the graduated scale: that is, the team that signed them was not required to give up much, because their salaries were under $150,000. Before the 1984–85 season there were only two players in the maximum compensation category ($200,000 and over), Glenn Anderson and Paul Coffey, both from the Edmonton Oilers. Rather than signing with other teams, these free agents elected to remain with Edmonton, which had won the Stanley Cup championship the year before.

Since 1982 the new agreement has not resulted in a major test of the new equalization rules at high levels of compensation, which is the most important indicator of the impact of free agency. The new rules have made it possible for more marginal players to change clubs and enhance their salaries, but the overall effect has not been great. This seems to be a financially healthy outcome for the NHL and its players. Teams spend substantial amounts of money developing their players. Players understand they are part of the business. Some teams would be unable to survive excessive free agency because of high salaries and difficulty of attracting a solid following by fans.

Overtime

Players in the NHL have a greater voice in policy decisions than those in any major professional team sport. The issue of overtime illustrates this participation. The overtime rule is important because public attraction to the game is enhanced by rules that create excitement. Until World War II, if there was a tie game at the end of regulation play, an overtime period was played to try to break the tie. But in 1942, the rule was eliminated because of wartime travel conditions. For four decades this practice continued in the NHL, although tie games in the Stanley Cup playoffs were broken by overtime. Few fans liked tie games, thinking them as exciting as "kissing your sister." A part of the old WHA's popularity with fans was that the league played ten-minute overtime periods. As the financial pressures on the NHL continued to mount during the 1970s, league officials began look-ing for ways to stimulate interest in the game.

By 1980 the NHL board of governors voted in favor of overtime if games were tied at the end of the regular three twenty-minute periods. But the NHLPA refused to agree to the proposal because it had not been consulted beforehand by the NHL. Although the NHL could probably have gone ahead with its decision anyway, it elected instead to wait for a consensus to emerge from among the players. During the 1981–82 negotiations, the issue was a lively topic of discussion. When the owners agreed to larger training camp allowances and increased per diems, the NHLPA agreed to waive their objections to overtime. In 1983 the board of governors took another vote and agreed to begin using a five-minute overtime period in the 1983–84 season. The new rule has worked out well. In the year before overtime was established, there were 127 tie games, about 15 percent of total games played. During the 1983–84 season, there were more tie games at the end of regulation play, 140, but 54 of these games were settled by sudden-death goals in overtime.

Antitrust Issues

Lawsuits over restraint of trade in hockey have challenged the drafting of players, the signing of NHL players by WHA teams, attempted relocation of the St. Louis Blues' franchise, and the rights to television broadcasting.

Player Draft

The player draft case is similar to and arose after the federal district court decision involving basketball player Spencer Haywood (see chapter 4). In 1976, a nineteen-year-old hockey player, Ken Linseman, signed a contract to play professionally with a team in the WHA. At the time, both the WHA and the NHL had a rule requiring that players be at least twenty years old to play in their leagues. When the WHA president voided the deal with Linseman, the player filed suit contending that he was the victim of an illegal restraint of trade under the Sherman Antitrust Act of 1890.[10] The court determined that the age rule harmed Linseman's career potential and constituted a concerted refusal to deal with him. Because the court struck down the age rule, the WHA and NHL lowered the age requirement to eighteen, and no further litigation has been brought challenging the new rule.

WHA

The World Hockey Association was established in 1971 by lawyer Gary Davidson, who had earlier formed the American Basketball Association as a rival to the NBA. Not since its birth in 1917 had the NHL confronted competition for players. At first, the NHL did not take the rival league seriously. But as players began to defect to the new league and it drafted talented players from the amateur ranks, the old league was forced to acknowledge that the battle lines had been drawn. Its first line of defense was to bring suit against players who jumped to the WHA.

The opening and decisive round in the litigation skirmish was fought when two valuable players for the Boston Bruins, Gary Cheevers and Derek Sanderson, signed contracts with WHA clubs. In favor of the NHL was a reserve clause, similar to that found at the time in other sports, which enabled the club to renew a player's contract into perpetuity. The Boston club sought use of the clause to restrain the two players from joining teams in the new league.[11] The players countered with the charge that the reserve clause violated the Sherman Act. Since the players' contracts with the Bruins were found to have expired at the time they were to play for their WHA teams, and because the reserve clause had not been reached through negotiations with the NHLPA, the federal district court denied the injunction request. Thus Cheevers and Sanderson were not restrained from joining their new WHA clubs. There were several other players who jumped leagues and became embroiled in litigation with the NHL. Although there was some variation in the issues involved, the antitrust laws were relied on to allow nearly all players who wanted to join WHA teams to do so if their contracts with NHL clubs had expired.[12]

By 1979, the NHL owners had suffered enough from the bidding war for players and the rapidly escalating salaries that it caused. In preceding years, the WHA had sent out feelers for merger, but the NHL was not then ready to come to terms. When finally the NHL board of governors and its WHA counterpart indicated their desire to merge, the players were not so willing. They saw further salary increases in a continuation of competition. NHL players threatened to sue the league as NBA players had done at the time of the NBA-ABA merger. At a crucial meeting between NHL owners and players, Alan Eagleson privately consulted with NHLPA president Phil Esposito, urging him to avoid costly litigation that might imperil weak teams and lose jobs for players. When Eagleson later reported to Esposito that the owners agreed to increase fringe benefits and allow the players to continue to enjoy the fruits of international hockey arrangements, Esposito recommended to the players that they accept the merger.

Thus in March 1979, the seven-year war between the rival leagues ended when the NHL agreed to absorb four WHA teams: the New England (now Hartford) Whalers, the Edmonton Oilers, the Winnipeg Jets, and the Quebec Nordiques. These teams paid $6 million each to join the NHL, and these funds were distributed to the old NHL clubs. The new NHL clubs were allowed to protect only two skaters and two goaltenders. The remainder of the players were made available to the old NHL clubs, with priorities established in cases in which NHL clubs had previously established rights to certain WHA players. To stock the new teams an expansion draft was held, with each of the old NHL clubs allowed to protect fifteen skaters and two goaltenders. In order to ward off future antitrust litigation with the NHLPA, the league described the agreement as an "expansion" rather than a "merger."

Franchise Movement

In April 1983, the St. Louis Blues were sold by the Ralston Purina Company to Coliseum Holdings Ltd. of Saskatoon, Saskatchewan, for $11.5 million. A local consortium had tried to buy the team, but was only able to offer $8 million. The Blues had lost an estimated $20 million in its six years of ownership by Ralston Purina.[13] At the time of the sale, questions were raised about whether the franchise would stay in St. Louis or move to Saskatoon, a city of only 165,000 people without a large hockey arena. As in other professional sports, franchise sales and movements are overseen by the NHL board of governors, which requires three-fourths approval of the owners represented on that board. The board voted to reject Ralston Purina's sale, which prompted the company to file a $20 million lawsuit in U.S. District Court in St. Louis against the NHL for restraint of trade in violation of the antitrust laws. Because awards in antitrust cases are trebled, the suit could effectively cost the NHL $60 million. If the federal courts were inclined to disallow a franchise move, this might well have been an appropriate situation in which to do it, because of the small population and lack of big league stadium facilities in Saskatoon.

In response to the legal action by Ralston Purina, the NHL filed a countersuit in June 1983, alleging that the company must operate the franchise for two more years before it can withdraw its ownership. The two years notice is required by the NHL constitution. In its suit, the NHL sought $3 million in damages plus punitive damages of $75 million or 5 percent of the assets of Ralston Purina, whichever is greater.[14] About two weeks after the suit was filed the NHL board of governors took over the Blues franchise from Ralston Purina, assuming control of all assets, in order to keep the club in St. Louis. This was another attempt to encourage the company to drop its antitrust action, because by taking over the club the NHL would assume responsibility for paying the company for its team. Subsequently, however, a sale of the team was arranged with California real estate entrepreneur, Harry Ornest. Meanwhile, the Canadian government's antitrust division began investigating the possibility of taking legal action on behalf of the province of Saskatchewan against the NHL for discrimination and conspiracy within a monopoly. Toward this end, the Supreme Court of Canada ordered the NHL owners to turn over their financial records to the Canadian antitrust division.[15] After several days of hearings in U.S. District Court in St. Louis, the parties reached an out of court settlement in 1985. The terms of the settlement were generally favorable to the NHL, which got the antitrust monkey off its back. Ralston Purina received $12 million, the same amount Ornest paid for the Blues.

Television Rights

Another equally complex series of antitrust suits involved a clash between large Canadian breweries, NHL clubs, and television companies. The so-called beer wars were over distribution of television revenues among clubs, and, like the St. Louis Blues litigation, threatened to split the league along United States and Canadian lines. Until recently, "Hockey Night in Canada" was the exclusive provider of NHL television broadcasts. While cable presentation of local games is growing rapidly, the twice-weekly national network telecasts by the Canadian Broadcasting Company (CBC) are still the predominant source of hockey coverage. These games are sponsored by the

Molson Breweries, which also owns the Montreal Canadiens. Along with the Canadiens, six other Canada-based hockey teams receive the lion's share of the several millions of dollars generated from the national telecasts.

The lawsuits arose because the fourteen United States–based clubs, which do not receive a proportionate share in the "Hockey Night" revenues, plus the Quebec Nordiques, which are owned by the rival Carling O'Keefe brewery, challenged the hegemony of the "Hockey Night" telecasts with their own television arrangement with Canadian Television, a CBC rival.[16] The television contract by the fifteen clubs was approved by the NHL for the 1984–85 season, and the lawsuits were subsequently settled by the parties.

A good argument can be made that it is in the interests of the long-run financial viability of the NHL to work out a more equal sharing of television revenues among teams. Professional football has practiced this for a long time, and recent agreements in basketball provide for revenue sharing. At present, baseball and hockey have some revenue sharing, but it is not equalized among clubs except insofar as the network baseball and ESPN hockey contracts are concerned. It is difficult to achieve parity and financial stability for all league teams in the face of widely disparate television revenues favoring teams in large metropolitan areas. What makes the problem so intractable in hockey is that the viewing audience in Canada is so much more loyal to hockey than the U.S. audience. But balancing out this circumstance is the fact that U.S. teams have a 2 to 1 majority over those based in Canada, so it seems likely that they will continue to battle for a greater share of Canadian television revenues because U.S. teams participate in these televised games.

Aberrant Behavior

Violence has always been a problem in the NHL. With players skating at speeds of up to thirty miles per hour, with sticks that can serve as weapons, and with a code of honor that condones roughhouse tactics, it is little wonder that players are susceptible to violence. Although many hockey players are beer drinkers and some players have had problems with excessive consumption, the problems of alcoholism do not appear to be significantly greater for them than the general population of males their age. Drugs are a relatively new thing to hockey players. Like their counterparts in other sports, many

141

have smoked marijuana. But serious drug abuse—substances like cocaine and heroin—has not been nearly as widespread in the NHL as in other major leagues.

Violence

In other team sports, most players lose respect for teammates who consistently pick fights or engage in other behavior aimed at injuring players on opposing teams. Violence in hockey is different in that it is often regarded as good strategy. Hockey players learn at a young age that they must face up to violence, that intimidation can be used to good effect.[17] For many years, officials in the NHL accepted fighting as part of the game, a kind of boys-will-be-boys approach. Fighting was penalized, but winked at as a problem. It was thought that the fans liked violence and that subduing the "enforcers" on teams would keep fans away from arenas.

Two developments have changed the conventional wisdom in recent years. One is the increased reliance on finesse that has come from awareness of the creativity, crisp passing, and quick transitions of the game as it is played in Europe and the Soviet Union. Victories by the smooth-skating foreigners in the Olympic games and Canada Cup events and an infusion of European hockey players into the NHL have caused a realization that the forceful brand of North American hockey is clumsy by comparison. The other development has been serious injuries to players caused by excessive violence in the NHL. Even though most players today wear protective headgear, they are vulnerable to debilitating injuries that can end careers.[18]

Under hockey's honor code, players who wish to fight drop their sticks and gloves and slug it out with bare fists. In the 1950s, for example, Gordie Howe of the Detroit Red Wings broke the nose of Lou Fontinato of the New York Rangers in a celebrated slugfest. During this era, there was rugged checking against the boards, clean contact in motion, and the occasional brawl between players. Malicious incidents increased during the 1960s and 1970s, especially as the Philadelphia Flyers, the most penalized team in hockey, rose to prominence with their bully-boy tactics. The game moved away from emphasis on skills to emphasis on intimidation, wrestling in the corners, and more acts of malicious intent to injure that resembled rugby or roller derby as much as hockey. With only three officials on hand to regulate this mayhem on ice, games frequently got out of hand. Sophisticated fans began to stay away.

Some remarkably ugly incidents occurred. In 1969, Wayne Maki of the St. Louis Blues struck Ted Green of the Boston Bruins on the head with his stick. This injury necessitated brain operations from which Green never fully recovered. In 1975, the Bruins' Dave Forbes launched a vicious attack on Henry Boucha of the Minnesota North Stars that included poking his stick into Boucha's eye. In 1978, Wilf Paiement of the Colorado Rockies swung his stick like a baseball bat against the head of Red Wings' player Dennis Polonich. In each of these cases the offending players were fined and suspended by the NHL—Maki for eleven games, Forbes for ten, and Paiement for fifteen. Polonich achieved an $850,000 verdict in court for his injuries. But, given the seriousness of these actions, the penalties imposed by the NHL were relatively light. Perhaps most symptomatic of the state that hockey was in is the case of Paul Mulvey of the Los Angeles Kings. When he was told by his coach to leave the bench to participate in a fight in 1982, Mulvey refused. As a result he was sent packing to the minor leagues. Reacting to this action against Mulvey, league president John Ziegler fined the Kings $5,000 and suspended coach Don Perry for fifteen days.

There are some signs that violence is finally beginning to decrease in the NHL. Average penalty minutes have declined somewhat, and the league has tightened up its rules on fighting.[19] For the 1982–83 season, a tough new rule provided that all players not involved in a fight must keep away, and stiffer fines were assessed to clubs (up to $5,000) and players who join a fight (at least $1,000 plus a three-game suspension). Rules were also established for punishing players that abuse officials. In 1983, for example, Tom Lysiak of the Chicago Black Hawks was given a twenty-game suspension for intentionally tripping a referee. In contrast, a similar offense a few years earlier by Paul Holmgren of the Flyers was punished only by a five-game suspension. Not coincidentally, with the NHL crackdown on violence, the quality of play has increased and so has attendance (table 5.1).

Drugs

Drug abuse is not extensive in the NHL. The league does not have a program for handling cases like the other three sports, but it has taken a hard line against offenders. In 1979, Don Murdoch of the New York Rangers was suspended for forty games after he tried to carry marijuana through Canadian customs. Montreal Canadiens player Ric Nattrass was arrested in 1981 for possession of two grams of hashish and one gram of marijuana. He was later fined $150 by a court in Canada. After the fine, which was usual in cases of this type, President Ziegler suspended Nattrass for a year, but he later reduced the suspension to thirty games. One other known incident involved a former NHL player, Steve Durbano, who was convicted in Canada for cocaine smuggling in 1984 and sentenced to seven years in prison. Durbano admitted using cocaine regularly when he played in the NHL, and estimated that 20 to 25 percent of the players are "doing drugs."[20] Based on the number of incidents reported among the five hundred players in the NHL, Durbano's estimate seems too high. On the other hand, the estimate could be reasonably accurate because it includes use of marijuana and speed as well as cocaine. Although hockey players are relatively uneducated as professional athletes go, they appear to recognize the dangers of using hard drugs. But, despite what seems to be a lower incidence of hard drug usage by hockey players, labor and management in the sport might do well to establish a drug control program along the lines of basketball and baseball.

6. *Past as Prologue*

The sports industry and its collective bargaining are in the midst of a transition period, the outcome of which will have a significant impact on the future viability of professional sports in America. In making predictions it is helpful to assess the significance of past events and the likelihood of their continuance in the future. For example, given the important effects that law and economics have had thus far, these variables can be expected to have still farther reaching influences on outcomes in professional sports, especially in terms of the rule-making process. Because of the newness and rapidly changing nature of industrial relations in sports, however, it is hazardous to simply extrapolate past developments to assess the future. Caution is necessary because the environment itself is unstable. This is evidenced by shifting social and public policies on sports, by the changes in the technological context of sports broadcasting, and by market constraints on team budgets and player incomes. The struggle for economic power between owners and players will doubtless continue. But whether it will involve increased hostility or greater cooperation between the parties is difficult to say for certain.

The games themselves are played in a relatively stable context. Rules of play are changed from time to time, but the sports retain a pattern that appeals to the audience's sense of continuity. The objective will always be putting points on the scoreboard. People like tradition and simplicity of outcomes. The intriguing nature and public appeal of sports are decisive to the overall success of the industry. Nevertheless, it is possible that the public's infatuation with spectator sports in general will wane, and as for the individual sports, popularity is even more variable. It depends to some extent on television exposure. Spectators can be fickle, shifting their enthusiasm from one sport to another. A sport may be "in" for a time, but then lose its allure.

Baseball has the advantage of a rich tradition, as the national pastime which fits in nicely with the rhythms of summer. Although the game is too slow for some, its measured pace and infinite variability are attractive to many. Football, the upstart sport that has challenged baseball by winning the hearts of countless fans, is unusually well suited to television. It provides the vicarious experience of controlled violence that appeals to the baser instincts of man. Basketball is also well adapted to television, displaying the subtle and artistic graces of exceptionally talented athletes. But the basketball season is long and demanding, and games suffer from the belief that only the last two minutes are decisive. Hockey has the violence element for thrill seekers, yet if cleanly played has a marvelous cadence that excites the mind with visions of crisp execution. However, hockey is the least suitable of the sports for television. Although a greater proportion of players are now American-bred, hockey is still considered largely a Canadian product.

With the rise in leisure time and discretionary incomes, it appears certain that professional sports will remain an important segment of the larger entertainment industry. As particular sports move into and out of mass popularity they prosper or decline economically. We think of the four major sports as continuing their dominance, but it may be that an emerging sport, such as indoor soccer, will capture the loyalty of a widespread audience in the future. Or perhaps an entirely new sport will be discovered by fans.

Commonality and Uniqueness

Each of the major professional team sports has characteristics common to the industry. At the same time, the individual sports face different constraints that affect economic health, making each sport to some extent unique economically. In terms of collective bargaining, certain structural features, strategies and tactics, and methods of dispute settlement are found in all sports. But each sport has developed variations on the basic collective bargaining model that are uniquely adapted to the needs of the actors.

Commonalities of Sports Models

In each sport, the actors in the industrial relations system can be clearly identified in terms of the labor-management-government model (figure 1.1). Players in all sports are organized into unions. The principal rationale for creating employee organizations is economic. Careers of players are short, and they recognize the importance of banding together to increase power vis-à-vis management. About four years is the average major league career of players in the NFL and NBA, and five years in the NHL. Although the average major league baseball player has a slightly longer career, players have a short time in which to maximize their incomes from sport. They realize that they are the ones providing the entertainment, and the games cannot go on without them. This fact of economic life means that players can generate significant bargaining power through the threat or use of pressure tactics.

Although the early unions in sports were poorly organized and relatively weak, as players became better educated and sought professional help from attorneys, negotiators, and agents, they developed cohesive structures to countervail the power of management. What took the players so long to break through and achieve substantial economic gains was the reserve clause found in the player contracts. These clauses bound the player to the club, thus limiting his bargaining power in the labor market. Baseball was the first sport in which players drove a wedge in the reserve clause and then later broke it entirely. The players gave back to management some control over their labor market mobility through collective bargaining, but baseball players are today more able to change teams voluntarily—and therefore use free agency to achieve higher salaries—than players in any of the professional team sports.

Management in professional sports consists primarily of individual entrepreneurs who own sports franchises and corporations that own teams. In the latter instance, ownership may be spread among numerous stockholders so the functions of ownership and management are more separate than when a single individual both owns and operates a team. In recent years, more individual owners have incorporated their sports franchises for tax purposes, but control remains in the hands of a single or a few individuals. Because of the importance of cable television, a growing number of sports franchises are being acquired by individuals or corporations that also have interests in the broadcast media. Ted Turner, the Atlanta-based owner of a cable television network, is probably the best example of this new kind of sports entrepreneur.

Although vertical integration may be the wave of the future in sports management and ownership, most franchises are not integrated operations; nor do the owners of teams constitute "big business" as regards their individual operations. Although the sports industry as a whole, especially when considered in terms of its relationship with television and the various satellite industries that derive income from sport, has become an important American industry, it is still dwarfed by industrial giants such as IBM or EXXON. In many respects, sports franchises are Mom-and-Pop businesses, and too frequently they are also operated that way. Professionalism of management in sports has been encouraged by increased television revenues, but for the most part, the labor relations function is professionalized only at the league level where collective bargaining takes place.

Augmenting the management of baseball, football, and basketball is the office of the commissioner. Hockey is the only sport that does not have a commissioner, although the NHL president carries out many of the functions performed by commissioners in the other sports. In recent years, the role of the commissioner has been strengthened considerably. Pete Rozelle became the dominant personality in football, and following his example, David Stern in basketball and Peter Ueberroth in baseball have emerged as vital spokesmen on television contract negotiations and other executive functions. Although Rozelle has not been directly involved in collective bargaining, the commissioners in basketball and baseball have exercised their influence to shape the outcomes of important agreements. Just as it is unwise for a corporate president or chief executive officer to be the principal negotiator in collective bargaining, so is it inappropriate for the commissioner to do so. The top manager is too vulnerable at the bargaining table and would have no backup authority figure. But he can become involved in various ways by keeping in close contact with the professional negotiator employed by the owners. Collective bargaining has become such an important aspect of professional sports that a commissioner must have expertise in labor relations and ability to influence negotiation outcomes. He ignores them at his peril. At the same time, however, the commissioner is expected to remain above the fray, aloof from the personal conflicts of negotiations, and to act as a public spokesperson on behalf of the sport, remaining unsullied. This is an exceptionally difficult role to play, and only the most astute executives can successfully walk the tightropes of the commissioner's office.

Government's role in sports industrial relations is varied and at times ambiguous. Despite all of the clamor and din of legislative soundings, there have been relatively few important new laws passed regulating the industry. The National Labor Relations Act, as amended, was well in place by the time that sports unions got around to utilizing its provisions. Its administrative agency, the National Labor Relations Board, has been active in trying to protect the rights of unions and players, but often its pronouncements have had little real impact on the relationships between labor and management. There has been some tinkering with the tax laws involving depreciation of players, but this too has not resulted in much fundamental change in industrial operation. Numerous bills to regulate professional sports have been defeated in Congress. Thus, on the legislative side, government has encroached little on the freedoms of the parties to carry out the mission of the industry and carve up the rewards through collective bargaining. Perhaps this is just as well, since excessive government regulation does little to promote economic growth and prosperity in any industry.

Government has taken a more activist and regulatory position in the judicial arena. To a large extent, the important battles affecting collective bargaining outcomes in baseball, football, and basketball have been waged in the courts. In all the professional sports, unions have secured protections from the courts in winning greater freedoms for players in the labor market. Even management has gained selectively, as in the case of Al Davis moving the Oakland Raiders to Los Angeles. Why the courts have exempted baseball from the application of the antitrust laws remains something of a mystery. Although there are still many contests yet to be staged, over issues such as drafting procedure, rights of amateur athletes, and free agency, a good argument can be made that the influence of the judicial system on sports will ultimately diminish. This has been the situation in other industries that have grown to rely less on legal measures as they mature. These industries have developed more sophisticated collective bargaining models and placed greater reliance on third-party neutrals in a private system of industrial jurisprudence. Whether sports can evolve toward such models, with reduced outside judicial influence, remains to be seen.

One aspect of negotiations that may well come under closer scrutiny by government is the role of agents. In representing players in individual salary discussions with team owners, agents have had a relatively free hand. It appears that they will be more heavily regulated in years to come. The football and basketball players' unions are now screening agents that represent their members. California recently passed the first state law regulating sports agents operating within a state.[1] Similar laws took effect in Oklahoma and Texas in 1985. Agents in California must file with the state labor commissioner an application along with affidavits of two persons vouching that the agent is of good moral character. Copies of agency contracts and fee schedules must be submitted to the labor commissioner for approval and a $10,000 surety bond posted. Agents must keep certain business records and have them available for inspection. Before contacting a student at a secondary or collegiate school in California, an agent must file a copy of his registration certificate with the school. Recent disclosures of agents tampering with amateur players who are not yet eligible for professional careers and mishandling of player funds by some agents may cause such laws to become more widespread.

Uniqueness of Individual Sports

Probably the two most dramatic signs of the acrimonious industrial relations in sports are the baseball strike of 1981 and the football strike of 1982. Both were full-scale walkouts that disrupted the regular season for lengthy periods. Strikes and strike threats are common in collective bargaining, especially in newly created formal relationships. But the strikes in these sports, as well as earlier, heated skirmishes between the parties, point up characteristics that distinguish baseball and football from basketball and hockey, which have never had player strikes. What is the difference between these sports that causes extreme hostility on the one hand and relatively peaceful negotiations on the other?

The difference is not explained by the collective bargaining structure, because all sports are characterized by multiemployer bargaining. Nor is it necessarily related to the stability of the industry itself or the potential for big money. One would expect to see more strikes in unstable segments of industry, yet basketball and hockey were probably more unstable than baseball and football when the strikes occurred; and basketball is the quintessential big money game for players. What appears to explain the difference in large part is the attitudes of the chief negotiators (selected by management and union), who have regarded negotiations as a potential bloodbath. High financial stakes from television were probably also part of the problem, but personality conflict between the chief negotiators made any kind of reasoned outcome short of a strike difficult to achieve. Now that there has been a changing of the guard of the chief negotiators in baseball and football, one would expect to see a more conciliatory attitude and less brandishing of swords for the benefit of the print and broadcast media, which only serves to heighten animosities and sharpen differences.

The unique feature of baseball is its exemption from the antitrust laws. Since 1922, baseball has enjoyed immunity from suits challenging the operation of the industry on restraint of trade grounds. Because of its monopoly control, professional sport in general is vulnerable to litigation over the impact of franchise allotment, player drafts, and pooling of revenues. That baseball has been relatively free from obstruction by government has in part explained its ability to expand operations and enjoy economic progress. There has, however, been relatively high turnover in franchise ownership. From 1969 to 1985, thirty baseball teams changed ownership. But in virtually all cases, the teams resold for more than what was paid for them. Despite record attendance levels in the two years after the strike, attendance fell off somewhat. Baseball ownership has become more risky, especially with the rapid escalation of salaries in recent years. Combined losses for the major leagues in 1983 were estimated at about $100 million, and many teams lost money in 1984 and 1985. Still, there is no shortage of willing buyers when teams come up for sale, and within the next five years, new franchises should be established in growing metropolitan areas that do not presently have major league baseball.

Baseball's newly liberalized system of free agency will be watched closely by leaders in other sports. Perhaps the most outstanding characteristic of baseball's collective bargaining agreement is the final-offer arbitration of salaries for players who elect to stay with their present teams. The owners have remonstrated for years about this provision, but they continue to include it in contracts. Arbitration grants equity through an impartial third party, and the final-offer feature helps to promote negotiations and elimination of extreme positions by the player and owner. Toting up for the several years this provision has been in effect, the ledger indicates that the number of cases won by players and owners is pretty evenly divided. Also, the provision has not been used excessively, which suggests that negotiation is doing its job well to resolve most salary disputes. It will be interesting to see if the extension of eligibility for salary arbitration from two years to three will result in the salary moderation the owners hope for. Following the precedent in basketball, baseball is facing up to the problem of dealing with chemical abuse problems among players.

There are some signs that the golden age of professional football is over. Television ratings for games in the NFL are down significantly, although there was some resurgence in 1985. From 1969–83, only four NFL franchises were sold. In 1984 and 1985, five teams were sold (Denver, Dallas, San Diego, Philadelphia, and New Orleans,) and several other owners have expressed a willingness to sell for the right price. NFL ownership remains a profitable venture, as the hefty prices in recent franchise sales indicate, but the USFL competition has pushed salaries upward at a fast pace, and the declining television ratings will temper the ability of the league to get a rich settlement with the networks (or cable) when the old contract expires at the end of the 1986 season. Should the USFL fail, which many observers predict, the NFL would be revitalized economically. Because football lacks general exemption from the antitrust laws, however, the league will continue to be plagued with suits on restraint of trade. Damages received by the Raiders' Al Davis from his successful litigation will take a heavy toll. Also, should the USFL win all or part of its $1.32 billion antitrust suit against the NFL, the older league's financial status would be in serious jeopardy. On the other hand, league expansion is planned and will generate additional revenues, and if the USFL folds, some of its teams may be incorporated within the NFL, which would add to league funds.

The hard line taken by owners in collective bargaining has paid off in the form of restricted free agency for players. With the advent of the USFL, this victory became less sweet because NFL players could readily jump leagues after playing out their contract options. Revenue sharing and screening of agents are the features in the NFL-NFLPA collective bargaining agreement that appear to be applicable to other sports or to industry as a whole.

As for basketball, it is too early to predict the full effect of the salary cap negotiated in 1983 on the economic health of the NBA, although it has good potential for stemming the losses suffered by many teams. Limited television exposure on the major networks has hurt the NBA. It is trying, with some success, to offset this limitation on revenues by greater exposure on cable stations.

Apart from the salary cap, there are two remarkable features resulting from negotiations between the NBA and NBPA. One is the profit sharing that provides an incentive for cooperation between labor and management to stimulate fan interest. This is the first use of profit sharing in professional sports, and other sports are likely to adopt similar provisions. To insulate franchises from wild swings in profitability caused by winning and losing seasons, a salary guarantee with additional income based on team profits makes sense for sports. Some kind of revenue sharing among teams is necessary to eliminate a have, have-not system in which teams in big cities dominate play and to make it less feasible for some teams to buy up an excess of talented players. Basketball's scheme may be a solution to this problem. The other significant feature of basketball that resulted from negotiations is the drug control program. This program recognizes the problem of chemical abuse and meets it head-on by encouraging treatment and punishing repeated violations.

Like basketball, hockey lacks exposure on U.S. television networks. Although hockey does have a source of growing revenue in American cable television, it has been without a network contract for several years. This severely crimps the economic growth of the sport, which is also vulnerable to antitrust challenges. The NHL, however, is showing signs of revival in attendance at games; it carefully nurtures its young stars for fan appeal; it no longer faces competition from a rival league; and it is curbing the excessive violence that has hurt its image.

Collective bargaining in hockey is commendable for its lack of confrontation tactics. Agreements reached are well reasoned and designed to suit the needs of the sport. In a practice similar to that in basketball, the executive director of the players' association is also an agent for purposes of representing players in individual salary negotiations. To some observers, this causes no harm or conflict of interest, but others question whether a union leader should be mixing roles and whether this does a disservice to the sport and players as a whole.

Players, through the union, have a strong voice in areas of traditional management policy. Cooperation between the parties has led to innovative uses of arbitration for settlement of free agency and salary disputes. Bargaining is unusual in the sense that the parties reopen contract provisions more frequently than in other sports. This is not necessarily adaptable for use elsewhere, especially in sports where each round of bargaining is fraught with a test of wills, but the system of frequent talks works well in hockey. This system will be tested again in late 1986, when the basic agreement expires. The players will rattle their sticks toward improvements in free agency and pensions.

Revised Bargaining Models

Conventional approaches to negotiation, which have been adopted in professional sports, regard it as an adversary proceeding, with each side contending for a greater share of the economic pie.[2] Models explaining the role of collective bargaining in sports have therefore concentrated on this conflict of interests and how best to resolve disputes between labor and management. In the future, the principal emphasis of improvements in sports bargaining will center on rationalizing the adversary model.

Adversary and Cooperative Models

The adversary model will be contrasted here with the cooperative model to illustrate their essential differences, and a synthesis of the two is suggested to make the adversary model better suited to the needs of the parties and the long-run prosperity of sports.

The adversary model, geared toward conflict, prescribes the acquisition, preservation, and protection of wage and nonwage objectives through negotiations. The parties' strategies in negotiations are effectuated through offensive tactics calculated to force the adversary to grant concessions and defensive tactics calculated to prevent the adversary from gaining concessions. In contrast, bargaining based on the cooperative model focuses on measures designed to increase the exploration of joint gain and the economic health of the industry. This approach invites the parties to go beyond the usual provisions of the negotiated agreement to establish programs that resolve problems of mutual interest. Instead of conducting negotiations in an atmosphere of crisis confrontation, the parties recognize and accept each other as partners in a cooperative venture. Rather than viewing negotiations as a contest, the parties pool their creative resources to devise new arrangements in which both sides recognize the need for mutual survival and sharing in financial rewards.

Given the traditional exercise of the adversary model throughout American industry, it was perhaps inevitable that the parties in sports would adhere to its precepts. But the results flowing from the application of this model to sports have not been encouraging. In the beginnings of the modern era of sports labor relations, from the late 1960s until the late 1970s, the adversary model was probably needed to make the owners realize that the industrial peonage of players could not continue. But the players have made their point, and further adherence to strong adversary positions is potentially damaging to the public image of sports and the stability of the industry. The sports unions may be able to continue to achieve generous economic gains through adversary tactics, but there is the risk of jeopardizing the ability of owners to operate successfully. Instability of franchises, especially when they not only change hands but move from city to city, destroys the tradition and continuity vital to the economic health of the industry. Over the longer term, both sides can lose if the public rebels against continued manifestations of greed.

A Synthesizing Model

In the past, management has preferred the adversary approach because of its fears that collaboration with players' unions would reduce its authority. These fears were well grounded because owner power was reduced by liberalized free agency and relinquishment of the lion's share of revenues. Sports unions, too, have viewed the adversary approach as consistent with their role as bargaining organizations and defenders of players' interests. They have been quite successful.

It does not seem likely that sports will be able to adapt to a full-scale cooperation model in the near future. It would be too much to expect that the unions would put aside their weapons and embrace management in widespread accommodation. But mutual survival of the industry depends more on future cooperation than on continuation of armed conflict. There are encouraging signs of a growing realization of joint interests and exploration of ways to enhance economic growth through greater cooperation. Good examples of this emerging recognition are the drug control programs in basketball and baseball, the salary cap and profit sharing in basketball, and in hockey, the ongoing communications between the union and management to resolve problems before they ripen into major disputes. Also encouraging is the growing use of third-party neutrals, mediators and arbitrators, to help resolve disputes when the parties are unable to reach agreement.

In the adversary mode the goal is to win. In the cooperative mode the goal is concession. A synthesis of the adversary and cooperative approaches would turn the goal away from simple domination or capitulation, toward achieving a reasoned outcome that serves the parties' mutual needs. This synthesis recognizes the essential competition between labor and management for shares of the economic pie, but maintains a commitment to cooperation in creative programs that increase the overall size of the pie. It makes joint labor-management programs to attract fan interest and promote industrial growth central to negotiations.

Outside neutrals fit into this model in two important ways. One is to help bring the parties together in reasoned agreement over complex bargaining issues. Mediation is a particularly suitable stimulus to negotiations. It has the advantage of allowing the parties to make up their own minds on the issues, yet assisting them with creative ideas, facilitating trade-offs, and drafting contract language. Once the agreements are formulated and converted to documentary form, arbitrators perform a second useful service, the interpretation and application of contract terms if the parties are unable to agree in earlier steps of their grievance procedures. This mechanism provides a private system of industrial jurisprudence that serves as an alternative to lengthy and costly courtroom litigation. It has proven successful for several decades in American industry, and a large body of useful precedent has evolved. More contract interpretation disputes—involving issues such as discipline, injuries, salaries, and enforcement of a variety of agreed-upon rules—are being resolved through arbitration. The scope of arbitration in sports is likely to continue to expand, with positive rather than negative effects.

Economics

The economic health of professional sport is closely linked to television. It will be even more so in the future. Existing leagues will expand, new leagues may form, and entirely new sports could evolve. But the common denominators of success in sports ventures are the extent of their television broadcasts and the ratings that broadcasts receive. Nearly all the other important economic elements of sport—player salaries, pensions and other fringe benefits, profitability of enterprises, profit sharing—depend in large part on television revenues. The United States is in the midst of a radical change in sports television broadcasting, which is occurring as a result of the growth of cable and pay television. The effect of this revolution in video entertainment is only beginning in terms of its impacts on sports. Although the eventual outcomes will remain unclear for some time, there are indications of the direction that they will take. It is likely that the most significant collective bargaining issue in sports will be how labor and management divide future television revenues. There is, however, less certainty about whether the bonanza that some expect will actually materialize.

Network Television

Table 6.1 shows the most popular television sports attractions, using a five-year average from 1979 through 1983. The number-one sport, in terms

Table 6.1   Network Television Ranking, Five-Year Average, 1979–83

Sport	Average Telecasts	Average Rating
Professional football	62.8	16.4
College football	24.2	11.1
"Wide World of Sports"	44.4	9.7
Boxing	17.4	8.5
Bowling	16.2	8.0
Major league baseball	23.6	7.2
College basketball	32.6	6.3
CBS "Sports Spectacular"	38.0	6.0
NBC "SportsWorld"	40.0	5.8
Professional basketball	12.2	5.8

Source: National Collegiate Athletic Association and A. C. Nielsen Co., as compiled by Sports Features Syndicate.

of the average number of telecasts and ratings, was professional football. Major league baseball ranked sixth and professional basketball tenth; hockey is not shown on network television in the United States.

Television contracts signed by the leagues with the networks in recent years have provided for substantial increases. But there are some indications that the size of future contracts will not show as healthy a growth rate as in the past. From 1980 to 1984, there was an industrywide decline of ratings for network sports programing of 15 percent.[3] Baseball and basketball ratings have held up reasonably well in recent years, but from 1981 to 1984, NFL football ratings fell by about 20 percent. The latter was in part due to over-saturation of football on television from USFL games and an increased number of college games, both on network and cable television. Lower television ratings mean lower advertising revenues for the networks, and should this trend continue, the NFL will not be in a strong bargaining position with the networks. The restructuring of the television marketplace does not bode well for the networks or for leagues that derive a substantial part of their incomes from this source. For this reason, there is speculation that the NFL may try to switch from network to cable television in whole or in part. A full-scale transition to cable at the end of 1986 seems unlikely, but the NFL could seek to broadcast home games of NFL teams on cable. There is added pressure on the NFL to negotiate sufficient revenues from television to keep pace with the league's expanding payroll.

Cable and Pay Television

While the 1960s and 1970s were the decades of network television, the 1980s has ushered in the era of cable and pay television. The latter may not displace network television as the dominant element of the broadcast media in the near future, but there is little doubt that it is here to stay and will be an increasingly competitive presence.

There is some confusion over the terms *cable* and *pay* television, because these terms are often used synonomously. *Cable* simply means that a coaxial, or special compound cable, is extended through underground channels to a location for sending television impulses. These impulses can be transmitted through the cable by a conventional transmitter or satellite. All cable services are paid for by viewers. In 1984, there were 33 million cable viewers in the United States, which constituted about 40 percent of the total television households.[4] *Pay cable* is a premium service offered to basic cable customers on a separate channel at extra cost (there is also a form of pay television that can provide signals to homes that do not have cable).

Pay cable television is the wave of the future for professional sports franchises. Basketball, baseball, and hockey have been particularly aggressive in arranging for contracts with pay television services. Table 6.2 shows cable revenues to the NBA for 1979 to 1986. The NBA has chosen to build the league's following in regional markets, where it is strong, rather than placing greatest emphasis on attracting a national network television audience, where exposure is limited and ratings are low (see table 6.1). Further evidence of the trend toward reliance on pay cable by the NBA is its 1984 agreement for $20 million with the Turner Broadcasting System, for national broadcast of fifty-five regular season and twenty playoff games in each of the next two NBA seasons.

The New York Yankees became baseball's pioneering regional pay television venture in 1978; however, the concept did not really catch on until 1984, when the San Diego Padres sold the team's broadcasting rights for forty games to Cox Communications for approximately $400,000. In the same year, viewers in fifteen states gained access to Sports Time, one of six new regional pay television services affiliated with eight major league baseball teams.[5] As a result of these new enterprises, for the first time more baseball games were shown on local pay television than on local free televi-

---

Table 6.2   NBA Cable Rights Revenues

Year	Revenues
1979–80	$400,000
1980–81	500,000
1981–82	900,000
1982–83	5,500,000
1983–84	5,500,000
1984–85	10,000,000
1985–86	10,000,000

Source: National Basketball Association.

sion (free television is something of a misnomer because advertising costs are passed on to consumers). Many major league teams have both free and pay television services available to local viewers, but the trend is clearly in the direction of fewer free games on local stations. As a result, the networks are showing concern over the encroachment on their markets. In 1984, in a move toward horizontal integration of its operation, ABC paid $202 million for the nation's most popular cable service, the Entertainment and Sports Programming Network (ESPN). ABC previously owned 15 percent of ESPN, which has a twenty-four-hour channel and 30 million subscribers.[6]

This market restructuring is having an already significant effect on revenues in the sports industry. But the future may hold even more dramatic changes. Suppose, for example, that the NFL or all four major professional sports leagues put up their own satellite to televise all games on a fee basis, a scenario dreaded by sports fans. If it happened, a segment of the entertainment industry would be created that would rival the film component in size. There are, however, reasons why it may not occur. One is that Congress might not allow pay television, which is relatively unregulated at present, to be used by the leagues for a profit cornucopia at the expense of the viewing public. Another is that there is still some uncertainty over the public's acceptance of pay television. If people have to pay for services that they are now getting free, they may not be willing to continue their sports viewing. There are fans who are so keen on their local teams and sports in general that they will pony up the added expense, as many are doing now. How far this market extends is an interesting question, one on which the future profitability of pay television and professional sports depends.

It appears likely that whatever the future success of pay television, it has already established something of a track record and this is having an effect on the disparity of team revenues. Teams in small population markets are simply not able to compete with those in large metropolitan areas that garner vast revenues from pay television. This accentuates the have, have-not disparity of teams in the acquisition of exceptionally talented players. With the extension of free agency, players can opt for teams in big-market locations, which can afford to pay higher salaries and load up with superstars. Basketball's collective bargaining agreement addresses this problem to some extent, as does football's corporate socialism of equal sharing of all television revenues by teams. But the vast profit potential from pay television may shatter the revenue sharing arrangements as owners in population centers seek to grab off a larger piece of the action. When Al Davis moved the Raiders from Oakland to Los Angeles, this is apparently what he had in mind.

Law

Much of the past strife between players and owners in professional sports has involved labor and antitrust issues stemming from longstanding practices like the reserve clause and drafting of players. The battleground is shifting to power struggles over who is going to get how much of the potentially enormous revenues generated by television.[7] As cable and pay television continue to allow deeper penetration into lucrative local markets, negotiation and litigation will increasingly focus on breaking old arrangements and forging new ones to exploit these markets. An interesting issue yet to be decided is whether the subject of television rights is a mandatory or permissive issue for bargaining. If this issue is determined to be mandatory, players will be more able to bring their power to bear on the distribution of proceeds. Even if television agreements are regarded as a management prerogative, and thus not an obligatory bargaining topic between labor and management, the sports unions will push for shared authority. Such a pattern has already emerged in hockey, where the head of the players' union has taken an active leadership role in arranging for television contracts that benefit the players.

Antitrust Issues

As labor and management mature and power is equalized, there will probably be less emphasis on antitrust litigation and increased attention to working out problems at the bargaining table and through the assistance of neutral third parties. Lawsuits have diminished in other areas of private industry and public employment as the parties develop greater reliance on their own resources for determining outcomes. Respect, trust, and accommodation take time to establish and require seasoned leaders at the helm. There are, however, several antitrust issues from the past that remain open to further litigation. One area of future courtroom conflict concerns new leagues. The USFL was established in large part as a television league, seeking to attract viewers during the spring. The expected television revenues never materialized, at least not in sufficient quantities, because of low ratings and limited exposure. The antitrust suit filed by the USFL against the NFL is at bottom a belated attempt to acquire television revenues forgone from lack of exposure. It seems unlikely that the USFL will prevail in this suit, but it could happen. If the damages awarded are anywhere near the amount that the USFL is seeking, they could bring the NFL close to bankruptcy.

Another area of continued antitrust action is franchise movement. The NBA's $25 million lawsuit against the San Diego Clippers, who moved to Los Angeles, is similar to the football litigation over the Oakland Raiders' move to Los Angeles. This issue also arose in hockey when the NHL refused to allow the St. Louis Blues to be sold to investors who wanted to move the team to Saskatoon, Saskatchewan. These lawsuits raise questions of the leagues' authority under antitrust law to prevent franchise movement. Although baseball has an exemption from antitrust law, it is possible that this exemption will not extend to relocation of franchises should a challenge arise. The Raiders' litigation would seem to put the question at rest by allowing free movement, but the federal appeals court in that case made reference to certain factors that a league can take into account in permitting a team to move, such as geographical balance, financial viability, population, economic projections, quality of facilities, and fan loyalty. Thus it appears that some franchise relocations may be blocked by the leagues, while others may not.

Baseball and basketball have had more team relocations than football and hockey (table 6.3).[8] Although there has been far more instability in sports franchises since the 1960s, this is due to the rise and fall of rival leagues and the teams in those leagues rather than movement of franchises within the previously established major leagues. Franchise movement is endemic in fledgling leagues such as the old American Basketball Association and the United States Football League. It cannot be said that the pace of franchise movement in the established major leagues has necessarily quickened in recent years, although there is a danger that this could happen in the future as a result of court decisions restricting league hegemony over where its teams operate.

The principal arguments in favor of allowing unrestricted movement of professional sports franchises begin with the need to uphold the sanctity of the free enterprise system. Although it is well known that leagues prefer to function as cartels that retain power over who is going to enter the business and where franchises are to be located, free markets are fundamental to capi-

Table 6.3   Franchise Movement Since 1953

	Baseball	Football (AFL/NFL)	Basketball	Hockey
1953	Boston to Milwaukee			
1954	St. Louis to Baltimore			
1955	Philadelphia to Kansas City			
1956			Milwaukee to St. Louis	
1958	Brooklyn to Los Angeles		Fort Wayne to Detroit	
	New York to San Francisco		Rochester to Cincinnati	
1960		Chicago to St. Louis		
1961	Washington to Minneapolis	Los Angeles to San Diego	Minneapolis to Los Angeles	
1963		Dallas to Kansas City	Philadelphia to San Francisco	
1964			Chicago to Baltimore	
			Syracuse to Philadelphia	
1966	Milwaukee to Atlanta			
1968	Kansas City to Oakland			
1969			St. Louis to Atlanta	
1970	Seattle to Milwaukee			
1972	Washington to Arlington, Tex.		San Diego to Houston	
1976				Kansas City to Colorado
1979			Buffalo to San Diego	
1980			New Orleans to Salt Lake City	Atlanta to Calgary
1982		Oakland to Los Angeles		Colorado to New Jersey
1984		Baltimore to Indianapolis	San Diego to Los Angeles	
1985			Kansas City to Sacramento	

Source: Paul D. Staudohar, "Team Relocation in Professional Sports," *Labor Law Journal* 36, no. 9 (September 1985): 729.

Note: Not included in the table are movements to stadium locations within the same metropolitan area, such as the Los Angeles Rams' move to Anaheim, California, or the New York Giants' move to a football stadium in New Jersey.

talism, and individual owners should have the right to determine the market area in which they will operate. Unrestricted franchise movement provides an opportunity for population growth areas to get franchises that they might not otherwise get. It also gives owners a greater opportunity to get out of cities that are not supporting their teams because of lack of interest or limited population growth.

Advocates further contend that the threat of departure by a team causes improvements in stadium facilities and may induce league expansion so that greater numbers of fans can enjoy live professional team sports. There is also a possibility that free movement of franchises injects new private capital into sports, i.e., new owners are willing to spend more on their teams if they have an ability to relocate readily.

Opponents of unrestrained franchise movement, on the other hand, contend that it introduces a risk factor into expenditure of public funds to finance stadiums. They also express cynicism over the unfairness of relocation because it deprives loyal fans of their teams. Franchise movement creates a large element of instability to leagues, team recognition, and players who would like to be settled with their families in an area. Cities are deprived of an important part of their economic base when teams leave.

Moreover, critics charge, free franchise movement exposes cities to a form of political blackmail: "Build a new stadium or improve existing facilities or we will move." Cities trying to lure professional franchises resort to enticements that exacerbate franchise hopscotch, and may themselves fall prey to the extortion game later on. It is further contended that excessive relocation hurts the overall public image of professional team sports, which is already beset with problems of drug abuse, declining television ratings, and fan resentment of high player salaries.

There are good arguments on both sides of the issue. No obvious solution to the problem seems indicated. It appears that a good case can be made for a compromise solution that gives the leagues some measure of control over franchise movement but which does not require a three-fourths vote by the league owners before a team can relocate. Basketball has reduced the requirement so that only a majority of owners is needed to grant approval. In addition, criteria for determining whether a franchise can move are needed to guide the decisions of owners. Greed is not a valid criterion, yet it was this factor that appears to have motivated Al Davis to move the Raiders out of Oakland, which had long supported the Raiders by sold-out crowds at games. Cities may have too great an emotional and financial stake in their stadiums and teams to be susceptible to losing their franchises simply because of a desire to heap larger profits on what is already a nicely profitable situation. If a team is clearly losing money because of lack of fan support, it should be able to change location.

In 1985, there were several bills in Congress that would prevent teams from moving at will. The most sweeping proposals were those introduced by Slade Gorton, senator from the state of Washington, and Senators John Danforth and Thomas Eagleton, both from Missouri. Features of these bills, which have been approved by the Senate Commerce Committee in 1984 and 1985, include (1) league approval of franchise movement, (2) consideration by the league of factors such as a team's profitability, playing facilities, fan support, and competition in the cities involved, and (3) that the league decision be approved by a board composed of a league representative, a person from the community threatened with a franchise loss, and a neutral party appointed by the American Arbitration Association. All the bills in Congress appear to allow a team to move if it can prove financial hardship at the present location.

This legislation is designed to protect cities and fans from greedy owners and mayors who ingratiate themselves with owners they are trying to attract to their cities. Passage in present form of any of the bills is unlikely, but pressure is mounting to develop rules to curb nomadic franchises. On the other hand, respect for the free enterprise system that allows owners to pursue their economic interests is a difficult obstacle to overcome. It is also questionable whether legislation can be developed that will satisfy the conflicting interests and put an end to further litigation.

It may be that Congress will be able to develop a compromise law that will limit franchise movement and place it on a more rational basis than what we have now. If so, it will require more careful evaluation of proposed franchise shifts to protect fans and cities. But Congress has been traditionally wary of passing laws affecting sports. If it fails to act, and perhaps even if it does pass a law, we have not seen the end of lawsuits over franchise movement. It may well be that the leagues will try to head off litigation by moving up their plans for expansion to additional cities.

What the future may hold is adoption by the courts of the eminent domain concept. This would recognize that sports franchises are too important to cities to allow indiscriminate relocation. Should such a concept be adopted, however, it would raise questions of how cities will come up with sufficient funds to allow them to buy a franchise, and how the price of a franchise would be determined in the first place.

What about extension of the Green Bay Packers concept? This professional football team is privately owned by a large number of citizens of that city who support the team and would not be likely to permit it to leave. A variation on this theme would be the creation of a quasi-private corporation, authorized by voters, city ordinance, or both to buy out the existing ownership. Virtually all the modern baseball stadiums, with the exception of Dodger Stadium in Los Angeles, are financed with public funds. Many indoor arenas are already publicly owned. It would thus be one more step in ownership to acquire the team itself. Shares of stock could be offered to the public in a franchise city. It is also possible that the city itself could be the sole or perhaps the majority owner and have the responsibility for overseeing the operation of the franchise. The city of Pittsburgh purchased a large share of the Pirates baseball team in 1985 to prevent franchise movement.

The city of Visalia in California currently owns a minor league baseball franchise. But extension of this concept to the major leagues presents difficulty in that all teams are privately owned, by individuals or corporations. The leagues and owners want to keep their businesses a private affair. So do the unions that represent players. Yet, the lamentable incidents in Oakland and Baltimore have aroused public indignation and prompted calls for a stop to franchise shifts motivated by cupidity. Should Congress choose not to set standards for team relocation, it is likely that creative financing through government will become a viable option in some cities.

Amateurs as Professionals

In recent years, the lines separating amateur and professional athletes have become blurred. It is likely that the future will see even more uncertainty over these distinctions. Some of the most interesting legal questions concern whether professional athletes can participate in contests previously open only to amateurs, such as the Olympic games, and whether amateurs can pursue professional interests. Several events contested at the summer Olympics in Los Angeles in 1984, including basketball and baseball, raised questions about professional eligibility. Such issues were also contended before the hockey competition at the winter games in Sarajevo. Willie Gault and Renaldo Nehemiah, who signed contracts to play football in the NFL, were also outstanding track athletes who sought to participate in the Los Angeles games. Their court actions to regain limited amateur eligibility were denied. This issue is likely to continue to pester sports because many amateur athletes already receive large sums for participation in events such as track and skiing, and the differences between amateur and professional exist in name only in many cases. There is a certain inequity associated with barring players from competition because of status that has little practical meaning.

Perhaps more important are the issues of players pursuing professional interests while maintaining a classification as amateur or college student. This is a fertile field for litigation and perhaps even unionization of amateur athletes. Numerous questions present difficult challenges to private and public policy. When Mike Rozier announced in 1984 that he had signed a contract with an agent and received payments during 1983, the year he won the Heisman Trophy playing football for the University of Nebraska, it sparked other revelations about such relationships that were prohibited by current rules. A leading agent representing football players indicated that more than a third of the nation's top players signed with agents in contravention of rules.[9] These disclosures have sparked charges of double standards and hypocrisy. Colleges prohibit players from negotiating their futures until their amateur eligibility has expired, yet they allow other students to contract with industrial recruiters while they are still enrolled — an inconsistency that is vulnerable to legal challenge as unjust discrimination against athletes.

College athletes are well aware that they are big revenue producers for their schools. Rules prohibiting their signing as professionals during their college careers rely largely on the protection of youth from exploitation and the value of a college education. Yet exploitation exists more in the value that players provide to colleges and the ready-made farm system that professional sports enjoy on a cost-free basis. Only about a third of football players earn college degrees, and many are spoon fed a pap of easy courses that have little real import for their future nonsports careers. Moreover, the big money exists for many top athletes not in college degrees but in professional sports contracts.

Some observers have suggested that, to remove the inequity and cynicism, colleges be allowed to establish teams that are semiprofessional, where players are paid openly for participation rather than under the table. Others advocate a union of college athletes that would actively pursue their economic interests. Although some would argue that college education and professional sports are antithetical, it seems likely that in the future they will be blended more. Although the exact nature that this mixture will assume is uncertain, the basic premise of denying an individual an opportunity to earn a livelihood will come under increasing fire. The premise will be challenged by attempts to strike down the exclusive drafting of athletes by single teams; to allow for relations with agents while athletes are still in school; to liberalize payments to college players; and to permit greater crossover between players from amateur to professional status, and vice versa.

Public Image

Virtually all productive enterprises depend on consumer markets for their viability and economic growth. Industries that produce goods and those that render services to the public tend to rise and fall in accordance with the consumer image of the attractiveness and reliability of their performance. Public image is especially crucial to the success of sports because the consumption of this service is based on a derived joy from entertainment rather than a biological need to sustain life. Dollars spent to view sports are from discretionary incomes, which can be allocated among various competing sources in the marketplace. Professional sport is a golden goose that feeds from a trough of monies supplied by the viewing public. Sport provides a world of myth and fantasy, but this world is not indestructible.

Illuminated by fantasy, sport is a world of players unspoiled by corruption. Contests staged on green fields, polished hardwood courts, and gleaming ice rinks reflect heroic deeds of forever youthful supermen. The games recall the playful, simpler times of spectators' own childhoods and help keep them young. But the myth is shaken by the rapacity of players and owners, the vitriol of their labor relations, and drug abuse among those so fortunate as to be big league athletes. Has the dream disappeared? How did sports slip from the age of innocence to the era of egoism? Have we seen too many games? These are questions being asked increasingly by sports fans.

The reality of professional sports has always been different from the myth. If cynicism with fallen heroes is on the rise, it is largely because their failures are more visible. The intense light of the media has exposed their humanity. Along with the drug issue, media attention has the greatest influence on the way the public perceives today's athletes. It shows players as little more than wealthy mercenaries with exceptional talents, which do not necessarily include emotional maturity. Still, there remain many true heroes among them. Owners have always been motivated by greed, but the sports business is more competitive and impersonal today. There are great men among the owners, but too often they are motivated by the quick buck and self-aggrandizement. Strikes, lawsuits, and holdouts have spoiled much of the fun.

To the extent that effective collective bargaining can help deal with problems that affect public image—drug abuse, strikes, and excessively high salaries—it can contribute to industrial success. In the past, collective bargaining has been as much a part of the problem as it has the solution. This is why the models of collective bargaining in the sports industry require change.

There are three principal behavior problems in professional sports: violence, gambling, and chemical abuse. Controlled violence is inherent in each of the sports covered in this book. Violence becomes aberrant when it goes beyond the rules of the games and threatens or causes malicious injury. Although violence is most commonly associated with football, the players are so well covered by protective gear that mischief leading to a lawsuit is relatively rare. Fights are endemic to football, but it is difficult to hurt someone wrapped in a shell of plastic. Hockey sticks and baseball bats are another matter, and so is the vulnerability of basketball players to a hard punch or kick. Violence could give rise to a special sports court that would determine fault and award damages. Bills for such a court or federal regulatory commission have been introduced in Congress.[10] Violence is currently handled by player fines and possible suspension or banishment from the game, with additional monetary remedy for players injured by violence sought in the existing civil or criminal courts. The high salaries of players have placed greater importance on forgone income from injuries caused by excessive violence. Accused players are represented in whole or in part by their unions, as they would be if accused of other forms of aberrant behavior. Judging from the relatively light penalties that have been handed out, unions have been effective in protecting players by mitigating punishment and hastening their reinstatement.

Because of the high salaries of players, risk of apprehension, and heavy penalties for violation, gambling has not been a serious problem in professional sports. All sports strictly prohibit betting on league games. Only occasional incidents have occurred, most recently involving Art Schlicter of the Baltimore Colts, who was suspended for the season by football commissioner Pete Rozelle.

Chemical abuse is a long-standing problem among athletes. In years past, alcohol took a heavy toll in shortening careers. Contemporary professional athletes have progressed from pill-popping to get up for games to the more serious aberration of cocaine abuse. It has been widely estimated that as many as 75 percent of NBA players have used cocaine at one time or another. High percentages have also been cited in football and baseball. Although the drug abuse problem has not been as visible in hockey, there have been incidents suggesting that it is not unknown to players of that sport. It is misleading to suggest, as Commissioner Rozelle once did, that drug abuse in sports is no greater than it is in society as a whole. Many athletes live in the fast lane, and all have the financial capability to acquire drugs. Reckless youth coupled with the pressures of achievement make players easy marks for addictive consumption of drugs. Cocaine, generally inaccessible in large quantities to less affluent sports fans, is viewed by the public as a hard drug. Its qualities are notoriously insidious and have arrested or ruined numerous players' careers. The rash of publicity attending drug busts and the revelation of drug habits among players have already done significant damage to the image of basketball, football, and baseball. To the credit of these sports, they are moving out of the dark ages of ignoring the problems toward recognition and assistance and finally to substantial treatment programs. The public need for vindication for perceived betrayal by sports heroes has been assuaged by tough penalties for repeat offenders and those who fail to come forward with problems.

In the not too distant future, all professional team sports will have comprehensive drug control programs that include testing. Observers who emphasize player rights on drug matters and who argue that what the players do is their own business, miss some basic points. Testing can only help the players, and the public image of sports is enhanced by removing the cloud of uncertainty over commitment to facing up to the problem. A societal problem of critical proportions, drug abuse is magnified in and by sports. If sport wants a good public image, it will have to earn it by presenting an example that is exemplary, not debilitating.

Thoughts on the Future

Various scenarios are possible for the future of sports. One major theme is that the relations between owners and players will remain rancorous, with strong adherence to adversary bargaining. Another is that the bargaining model will be characterized by cooperation, with joint problem solving rather than a test of wills. It seems probable that the future will see an admixture of these models, with adversary bargaining tempered by a gradual shift in the direction of accommodation on areas of mutual concern. Labor and management in professional sports cannot simply continue to pursue their own ends without concern for the effects of their decisions on the public. Fan support determines the bottom line of successful operation, and arrangements worked out between labor and management will have to recognize the need to preserve the public image. Government regulation may help to rationalize industrial operation in certain areas where the parties are unable or unwilling to come to grips with problems, but the future health of the industry is going to be influenced in major part by what the parties do to resolve emerging problems.

Success implies a balancing of interests and a recognition of the need for mutual survival. For example, the NBA's sharing of pay television revenues should allow for increased competitive balance among teams, the ultimate result of which should be greater prosperity for owners and players. It is not corporate socialism but a kind of player-induced socialism-for-all that seems likely to emerge. The inherent instability of professional sports operation suggests the need for basing salary structures more on profit sharing than on the ability of individual players to command higher salaries. What may emerge is a narrowing of the dispersion between player salaries, perhaps through establishment of salary scales that reflect seniority, with wages above scale determined by team or league profits. This implies a reduced role for agents, although their complete disappearance is unlikely to occur in the foreseeable future. On the other hand, greed may prevent such arrangements from more widespread adoption, and the sports industry may move toward a free market approach based on survival of the fittest. What argues against this latter course is the destruction of competitive balance that could diminish fan interest and contract the market potential for the leagues as a whole.

There is no doubt that unions have been extraordinarily successful in enhancing the economic status of players. A question arises as to whether this success may sow the seeds of future problems in the growth and stability of the industry. If we look at the automobile, steel, airline, and trucking industries, we see a string of union successes that was later broken by industrial decline and restructuring. Could this happen in sports? Perhaps, but not for the same reasons. The decline of certain heavily unionized American industries has been the result of foreign and domestic competition, with the latter caused by deregulation. American professional team sports do not face foreign competition except in the limited sense of European soccer games on television. Since sports are not now heavily regulated, deregulation would not create domestic competition. But competition does exist from nonindustrial components. For instance, the fitness revolution has caused more active participation in sports, and many persons now do this as an alternative to being spectators. The decline in network television ratings of professional sports suggests that the industry is not immune from competition. There are many other entertainment choices that compete with sports. Some observers have argued that the big strikes in baseball and football have turned off the fans. Although this is not corroborated by attendance levels, a good case can be made that future lengthy strikes present a more significant risk to fan loyalty.

Despite the past success of the professional sports industry in America, a growing number of observers are worried about the future. During the 1970s, the number of sports heroes who were revered as much for their dignity as for their achievements on the playing field declined. Who inspired noble actions in society, especially among young people? Where have you gone Joe DiMaggio, Stan Musial, Lou Gehrig, Joe Louis, Connie Mack, Red Grange, Elgin Baylor? Today's professional athletes are celebrities that achieve notoriety more for their media images and cupidity than for their playing skills and personal integrity.[11] It is little wonder that many fans have lost their appetite for the seemingly endless parade of superstars that the media-sports complex churns out. To these fans, the whole of sports is becoming increasingly banal. They feel alienated because the games and players seem to be meant less for them and more for promoting the business of sport as a haven for the privileged participants.[12] The boundaries defining professional sports are becoming blurred and seem carelessly mingled into a shadowy kind of "moneyball." This change is part of a general shift in American society, away from a sense of common identity rooted in tradition and toward emphasis on economic achievement based on individualism.

While there are some signs that the industry is leveling off its growth curve, there are no obvious indications that it will not have a reasonably prosperous future. The degree to which this prosperity is realized will depend largely on the growth of television viewing, especially on a pay basis, and the extent to which labor and management can work out problems of mutual concern in collective bargaining. Heated conflicts in negotiations seem to be on the decline. Drug abuse issues have subsided, although they will continue to surface. The future will not likely be one of unparalleled growth in professional sports. Many problems will persist, and new ones will arise. But sports should remain a vibrant industry that brings much satisfaction to the public.

Notes

1. Introduction

1. This quotation, perhaps apocryphal like some other words and gestures attributed to the colorful Babe, is cited in Dale Yoder and Paul D. Staudohar, *Personnel Management and Industrial Relations*, 7th ed. (Englewood Cliffs, N. J.: Prentice-Hall, 1982), 332. In addition to this textbook, the reader who is generally unfamiliar with the industrial relations literature should see especially Gordon F. Bloom and Herbert R. Northrup, *Economics of Labor Relations*, 9th ed. (Homewood, Ill.: Richard D. Irwin, 1981); Neil W. Chamberlain, Donald E. Cullen, and David Lewin, *The Labor Sector*, 3d ed. (New York: McGraw-Hill, 1980); Robert E. Allen and Timothy J. Keaveny, *Contemporary Labor Relations* (Reading, Mass.: Addison-Wesley Publishing Company, 1983); Thomas A. Kochan, *Collective Bargaining and Industrial Relations: From Theory to Policy and Practice* (Homewood, Ill.: Richard D. Irwin, Inc., 1980); and William H. Holley and Kenneth M. Jennings, *The Labor Relations Process*, 2d ed. (Chicago: Dryden Press, 1984).

2. Marie Hart and Susan Birrell, eds., *Sport and the Sociocultural Process*, 3d ed. (Dubuque, Iowa: Wm. C. Brown Company Publishers, 1981), x.

3. A good reference on this subject is Johan Huizinga, *Homo Ludens: A Study of the Play Element in Culture* (Boston: Beacon Press, 1950).

4. For another view, see Douglas A. Noverr and Lawrence E. Ziewacz, *The Games They Played: Sports in American History, 1865–1980* (Chicago: Nelson-Hall, 1983).

5. John T. Dunlop, *Industrial Relations Systems* (New York: Henry Holt and Company, 1958).

6. For a separate model based on this idea, see Thomas A. Kochan, Robert B. McKersie, and Peter Cappelli, "Strategic Choice and Industrial Relations Theory," *Industrial Relations* 23, no. 1 (Winter 1984): 16–39.

7. David Tajgman, "A Primer of Labor Relations in the Entertainment Industry," *ILR Report* (New York State School of Industrial and Labor Relations, Cornell University) 21, no. 2 (Spring 1984): 8.

8. This definition is adapted from Jack Barbash, *The Elements of Industrial Relations* (Madison, Wis.: University of Wisconsin Press, 1984).

9. Portions of this discussion are from Robert C. Berry, William B. Gould IV, and Paul D. Staudohar, *Labor Relations in Professional Sports* (Dover, Mass.: Auburn House Publishing Company, 1986), 31–32, and are reprinted here with the permission of the publisher.

10. Yoder and Staudohar, *Personnel Management and Industrial Relations*, 477.

11. Barbash, *Elements of Industrial Relations*, 6.

2. Baseball

1. For a good discussion of the unique characteristics of baseball as an economic enterprise, see Jesse W. Markham and Paul V. Teplitz, *Baseball Economics and Public Policy* (Lexington, Mass.: Lexington Books, 1981), 17–33.

2. Interestingly, the economics literature maintains that a labor market with monopolistic control by owners would lead to the same allocation of players and team strengths as would occur if the labor market were competitive. Only the distribution of wealth between the players and owners would be affected. See Joseph W. Hunt, Jr., and Kenneth A. Lewis, "Dominance, Recontracting, and the Reserve Clause: Major League Baseball," *American Economic Review* 66, no. 5 (December 1976): 936.

3. Figures from Sports Business Research, cited in *Wall Street Journal*, 21 October 1983, 17.

4. *American League of Professional Baseball Clubs*, 180 NLRB 189 (1969).

5. *Federal Baseball Club* v. *National League*, 259 U.S. 200 (1922).

6. *Flood* v. *Kuhn*, 407 U.S. 258 (1972). See also *Toolson* v. *New York Yankees*, 346 U.S. 356 (1953).

7. Some of the material in this section is from Paul D. Staudohar, "Player Salary Issues in Major League Baseball," *Arbitration Journal* 33, no. 4 (December 1978): 17–18.

8. For a profile of Miller's background, see Robert H. Boyle, "This Miller Admits He's a Grind," *Sports Illustrated*, 11 March 1974, 22–26.

9. Murray Chass, "Player Union Fires Moffett for 'Soft Line'," *Sporting News*, 5 December 1983.

10. Murray Chass, "Moffett Links Dismissal to Disputes with Miller," *New York Times*, 24 November 1983, 20.

11. These factors are analyzed quantitatively in Gerald W. Scully, "Pay and Performance in Major League Baseball," *American Economic Review* 64, no. 6 (December 1974): 915–30.

12. Paul Blustein, "Are Baltimore Orioles Best Team in Baseball Or Just the Best Run?" *Wall Street Journal*, 5 October 1983, 1, 16.

13. Materials in this section are based on Paul D. Staudohar and Edward M. Smith, "The Impact of Free Agency on Baseball Salaries," *Compensation Review* 13, no. 3 (Third Quarter 1981): 51–52.

14. Data from *Sports Illustrated*, 5 December 1977, 15.

15. Murray Chass, "Baseball Ratings: Fodder for Arguments," *Sporting News*, 7 November 1983, 58.

16. James Richard Hill and William Spellman, "Professional Baseball: The Reserve Clause and Salary Structure," *Industrial Relations* 22, no. 1 (Winter 1983): 16.

17. Henry J. Raimondo, "Free Agents' Impact on the Labor Market for Baseball Players," *Journal of Labor Research* 4, no. 2 (Spring 1983): 192.

18. This study found that of players inducted into the Hall of Fame, only 22 percent played their entire careers with just one team, compared with 32 percent of active players with a chance of making the Hall of Fame. See *Sports Illustrated*, 22 November 1982, 22.

19. Dale Yoder and Paul D. Staudohar, *Personnel Management and Industrial Relations*, 7th ed. (Englewood Cliffs, N.J.: Prentice-Hall, Inc., 1982), 488.

20. James B. Dworkin, *Owners Versus Players: Baseball and Collective Bargaining* (Boston: Auburn House Publishing Company, 1981), 153.

21. C. Raymond Grebey, Jr., "Another Look at Baseball's Salary Arbitration," *Arbitration Journal* 38, no. 4 (December 1983): 27.

22. National Institute on Drug Abuse, *Drug Use in Industry*, Services Research Report, Alcohol, Drug Abuse and Mental Health Administration (Washington, D.C.: U.S. Government Printing Office, 1979), p. 11. See also Harrison M. Trice and Paul M. Roman, *Spirits and Demons at Work: Alcohol and Other Drugs on the Job*, 2d ed. (Ithaca, N.Y.: New York State School of Industrial and Labor Relations, Cornell University, 1978); and Tia Schneider Denenberg and R. V. Denenberg, *Alcohol and Drugs: Issues in the Workplace* (Washington, D.C.: The Bureau of National Affairs, Inc., 1983).

23. According to one source, from 1981 to the start of the 1984 season twenty players admitted using or were caught using or possessing drugs, or admitted to being alcoholics. See *Sports Illustrated*, 26 March 1984, 9.

24. Frederick Klein, "Baseball: Time to Talk Turkey," *Wall Street Journal*, 2 November 1984, 20.

25. Murray Chass, "The Days Dwindle down to a Precious Few," *Sporting News*, 22 July 1985, 45.

26. Walt Gibbs, "The Man the Baseball Owners Love to Hate," *San Francisco Sunday Examiner and Chronicle*, 21 July 1985, C2.

3. Football

1. Good sources on the origins of professional football are Gene Brown, editor, *The New York Times Encyclopedia of Sports*, vol. 1, *Football*, with introduction by Frank Litsky (New York: Arno Press, 1979); and Douglas A. Noverr and Lawrence E. Ziewacz, *The Games They Played: Sports in American History, 1865–1980* (Chicago: Nelson-Hall, 1983), 83–87.

2. Portions of this discussion are based on Paul D. Staudohar, "Professional Football and the Great Salary Dispute," *Personnel Journal* 61, no. 9 (September 1982): 673–79.

3. *National Football League Management Council and National Football League Players Association*, 203 NLRB 165 (1973), 83 LRRM 1203 (1973).

4. "NFL Owners Told to Bargain on Rules That Involve Safety," *Wall Street Journal*, 26 July 1976, 25.

5. *NFL Players Association v. NLRB*, 503 F.2d 12 (1974), 87 LRRM 2118 (1974).

6. Collective Bargaining Agreement between National Football League Players Association and National Football League Management Council, 1977, 8.

7. Collective Bargaining Agreement between National Football League Players Association and National Football League Management Council, 1982, 32–33.

8. Letter from Frank Woschitz, director, public relations, NFLPA, to the author, December 7, 1984.

9. Ira Miller, "Upshaw's Line Isn't Offensive," *San Francisco Chronicle*, 14 September 1983, 67.

10. Dennis A. Ahlburg and James B. Dworkin, "Player Compensation in the National Football League: An Empirical Analysis," Working Paper 83-04, Industrial Relations Center, University of Minnesota, January 1983, 5–6.

11. "The Cherry on Top," Scorecard, ed. by Jerry Kirshenbaum, *Sports Illustrated*, 19 March 1984, 15.

12. Joanne Lipman, "USFL Owners Exude Confidence Despite League's First-Year Loss," *Wall Street Journal*, 14 July 1983, 29.

13. Discussion of the reserve clause is found in Edward R. Garvey, "From Chattel to Employee: The Athlete's Quest for Freedom and Dignity," *The Annals of the American Academy of Political Science*, no. 445 (September 1979): 92–95.

14. *Radovich v. NFL*, 352 U.S. 445 (1957).

15. *Kapp v. National Football League*, 390 F.Supp. 73 (1974), *aff'd*, 586 F.2d 644 (9th Cir. 1978), *cert. denied*, 441 U.S. 907 (1979).

16. *Mackey* v. *National Football League*, 543 F.2d 644 (8th Cir. 1976), *cert. dismissed*, 434 U.S. 801 (1977). For further discussion of the *Kapp* and *Mackey* cases, see Steven M. Strauss, "Sport in Court: The Legality of Professional Football's System of Reserve and Compensation," *UCLA Law Review* 28, no. 2 (December 1980): 252–90.

17. Frank A. Scott, Jr., James E. Long, and Ken Somppi, "Free Agency, Owner Incentives, and the National Football League Players Association," *Journal of Labor Research* 4, no. 3 (Summer 1983): 257–64.

18. *Smith* v. *Pro Football, Inc.*, 420 F.Supp. 738, 593 F.2d 1173 (1978).

19. Robert B. Terry, "Application of Antitrust Laws to Professional Sports' Eligibility and Draft Rules," *Missouri Law Review* 46, no. 4 (Fall 1981): 797–828.

20. Jerry Kirshenbaum, "Exploitive and Collusive," *Sports Illustrated*, 7 March 1983, 19.

21. *NFL et al.* v. *Oakland Raiders et al; Oakland-Alameda County Coliseum* v. *Oakland Raiders et al.*, 105 S. Ct. 397 (1984).

22. *City of Oakland* v. *Oakland Raiders*, 646 P. 2d 835 (1982).

23. Neil Amdur, "NFL to Check Redskins on Drug Report," *New York Times*, 15 November 1973.

24. "Report NFL Cocaine Use Now 50 Percent," *San Francisco Sunday Examiner and Chronicle*, 14 August 1983, C6.

25. "Four Players Suspended by Rozelle for Drug Use," *Los Angeles Times*, 26 July 1983, part 3, 1.

4. Basketball

1. For detailed discussion of the origins of basketball, see Glenn Dickey, *The History of Professional Basketball since 1896* (New York: Stein and Day Publishers, 1982), 3–9; Douglas A. Noverr and Lawrence E. Ziewacz, *The Games They Played: Sports in American History, 1865–1980* (Chicago: Nelson-Hall, 1983), 31–32; and *The New York Times Encyclopedia of Sports*, vol. 3, *Basketball*, ed. by Gene Brown with introduction by Frank Litsky (New York: Arno Press, 1979).

2. Roger G. Noll and Benjamin A. Okner, *The Economics of Professional Basketball*, reprint no. 258 (Washington, D.C.: Brookings Institution, 1973), 2.

3. David DuPree, "NBA: Red Ink and a Bleak Future," *Washington Post*, 15 March 1983, D4.

4. The original ABL teams were located in Cleveland, New York, Kansas City, Pittsburgh, Chicago, Hawaii, and San Francisco.

5. Dickey, *History of Professional Basketball*, 142.

6. Al Harvin, "A.B.A. Owners Agree to Pay $11-Million Merger Indemnity," *New York Times*, 15 April 1970, 58.

7. Michael S. Jacobs and Ralph K. Winter, Jr., "Antitrust Principles and Collective Bargaining by Athletes: Of Superstars in Peonage," *Yale Law Journal* 81, no. 1 (November 1971): 5.

8. Gerald W. Scully, "Economic Discrimination in Professional Sports," *Law and Contemporary Problems* 38 (Winter-Spring 1973): 68.

9. *The Modern Encyclopedia of Basketball*, ed. by Zander Hollander (New York: Four Winds Press, 1969), 218.

10. Damon Stetson, "N.B.A. Acts to Bar Racial Incidents," *New York Times*, 23 January 1959, 15.

11. "Cousy to Discuss Union with Labor Executive," *New York Times*, 13 January 1957, sec. 5, 9.

12. Erwin G. Krasnow and Herman M. Levy, "Unionization and Professional Sports," *Georgetown Law Journal* 51, no. 4 (Summer 1963): 764.

13. Leonard Koppett, "N.B.A. Players Threaten Strike in Dispute over Pension Plan," *New York Times*, 15 January 1964, 34.

14. Ray Kennedy and Nancy Williamson, "Money: The Monster Threatening Sports," *Sports Illustrated*, 17 July 1978, 52.

15. "N.B.A. Money," *New York Times*, 24 March 1983, sec. 2, 16.

16. 147 F.Supp. 154 (1956).

17. 389 F.Supp. 867 (1975).

18. *Central New York Basketball, Inc.* v. *Barnett*, 181 N.E.2d 506 (1961).

19. *Minnesota Muskies* v. *Hudson*, 294 F.Supp. 979 (1969).

20. *Washington Capitols Basketball Club, Inc.* v. *Barry*, 419 F.2d 472 (9th Cir.), which affirmed 304 F.Supp. 1183 (N.D. Cal. 1969).

21. *Lemat Corporation* v. *Barry*, 80 Cal. Rptr. 240 (1969).

22. The case that eventually resulted from the chain of events that occurred is *Denver Rockets* v. *All-Pro Management, Inc.*, 325 F.Supp. 1049 (C.D. Cal. 1971).

23. Ibid., 1055.

24. *Levin* v. *National Basketball Association*, 385 F.Supp. 149 (1974).

25. *Robertson* v. *National Basketball Association*, 389 F. Supp. 867 (1975). The *Robertson* case is discussed in Leslie Michele Lava, "The Battle of the Superstars: Player Restraints in Professional Team Sports," *University of Florida Law Review* 32, no. 3 (Spring 1980): 683–86; and Michael S. Hobel, "Application of the Labor Exemption after the Expiration of Collective Bargaining Agreements in Professional Sports," *New York Law Review* 57, no. 1 (April 1982): 164–202.

26. *Robertson* v. *National Basketball Association*, 72 F.R.D. 64, S.D.N.Y. (1976), aff'd, 556 F.2d 682 (2d Cir. 1977).

27. John C. Weistart, "Judicial Review of Labor Agreements: Lessons from the Sports Industry," *Law and Contemporary Problems* 44, no. 4 (Autumn 1981): 135.

28. *Matter of Robertson Class Plaintiffs*, 479 F. Supp. 657 (S.D.N.Y. 1979).

29. *Robertson Class Plaintiffs* v. *National Basketball Association*, 625 F. 2d 407, 416 (2d Cir. 1980).

30. Sam Goldaper, "Knicks Are Upheld on King Offer Sheet," *New York Times*, 9 October 1982, 22.

31. The dispute was settled by establishment of an annual pay scale for referees of $28,000 for beginners up to $85,000 for those with sixteen years experience. See "NBA's Lockout of Officials Ends with Settlement," *Los Angeles Times*, 10 December 1983, pt. III, 1.

32. Sam Goldaper, "Owner Dares N.B.A. Union to Strike," *New York Times*, 18 February 1983, 26.

33. "Pay the Pacer, Call the Tune," *Sports Illustrated*, 11 April 1983, 13.

34. *Molinas* v. *Podoloff*, 133 N.Y.S. 2d 743 (1954).

35. *Saunders* v. *National Basketball Association*, 348 F. Supp. 649 (N.D. Illinois 1972).

36. Curry Kirkpatrick, "Shattered and Shaken," *Sports Illustrated*, 2 January 1978, 46; and John F. Carroll, "Torts in Sports—'I'll See You in Court'!" *Akron Law Review* 16, no. 3 (Winter 1983): 537–53.

37. Barbara Hink, "Compensating Injured Professional Athletes: The Mystique of Sports Versus Traditional Sports Principles," *New York University Law Review* 55, no. 5 (November 1980): 973.

5.   Hockey

1. Gene Brown, ed., *The New York Times Encyclopedia of Sports*, vol. 8, *Soccer/Professional Hockey* (New York: Arno Press, 1979), 213.

2. Data reported in *Wall Street Journal*, 9 December 1983, 16.

3. Data from *Wall Street Journal*, 1 January 1984, 27.

4. In October 1983, the median salary for goaltenders was $130,000, for defensemen $120,000, and for forwards $114,000. Data from NHLPA salary survey.

5. While player contributions are not required, voluntary payments may be made into the pension fund to increase a player's share.

6. Although Junior A players are considered amateurs for most purposes, the National Collegiate Athletic Association in the United States regards Tier One Junior A players as professionals because they receive money and room and board for their services.

7. Data from *Sporting News*, 11 November 1985, 45.

8. *McCourt* v. *California Sports, Inc.*, 600 F. 2d 1193 (1979). See also Mark S. Miller, "The National Hockey League's Faceoff with Antitrust: McCourt v. California Sports, Inc.," *Ohio State Law Journal*, 42, no. 2 (1981): 603–26.

9. Data from *Sporting News*, 22 August 1983, 49; and 16 July 1984, 48.

10. *Linseman* v. *World Hockey Association*, 439 F. Supp. 1315 (1977).

11. *Boston Professional Hockey Ass'n, Inc.* v. *Cheevers*, 348 F. Supp. 261, *remanded*, 472 F. 2d 127 (1972).

12. See, for example, *Nassau Sports* v. *Hampson*, 355 F. Supp. 733 (1972); and *Philadelphia World Hockey Club* v. *Philadelphia Hockey Club*, 351 F. Supp. 462 (1972). In one of these cases, however, a player whose contract had expired was not allowed to change leagues until a one-year option renewal elapsed, *Nassau Sports* v. *Peters*, 352 F. Supp. 870 (1972).

13. "Blues Sue N.H.L. in Antitrust Action," *New York Times*, 25 May 1983, B7.

14. "Countersuit by N.H.L. over Blues," *New York Times*, 19 June 1983, A25.

15. *Los Angeles Times*, 9 March 1984, pt. III, 6.

16. Gerald Eskenazi, "Suits over TV Split N.H.L.," *New York Times*, 17 August 1984, A17.

17. See Edmund W. Vaz, *The Professionalization of Young Hockey Players* (Lincoln, Neb.: University of Nebraska Press, 1982).

18. In 1979, the NHL board of governors voted to require all players to wear helmets. The NHLPA, however, vetoed the proposed rule because some players felt uncomfortable wearing helmets. In a compromise rule, all players entering the NHL after June 1979 must wear helmets. In the 1985–86 season, only a handful of players continued to play bareheaded.

19. Average penalty minutes per game reached a peak in the 1980–81 season at 41.5. In 1981–82, the average was 40.2; in 1982–83, it dropped to 33.8; in 1983–84, it was at 36.4; and in 1984–85, it was 37.4. Data provided by the NHL.

20. "Durbano in Prison, Says NHL Has a Drug Problem," *Los Angeles Times*, 19 March 1984, pt. III, 8.

6. Past as Prologue

1. This law is further discussed in Phillip J. Closius, "Not at the Behest of Nonlabor Groups: A Revised Prognosis for a Maturing Sports Industry," *Boston College Law Review* 24, no. 2 (March 1983): 397–98.

2. For a more detailed discussion of the ideas in this section, see Dale Yoder and Paul D. Staudohar, "Rethinking the Role of Collective Bargaining," *Labor Law Journal* 34, no. 5 (May 1983): 311–16; and Roger Fisher and William Ury, *Getting to Yes: Negotiating Agreement without Giving In* (Boston: Houghton Mifflin, 1981).

3. William Taaffe, "Howard, the Guys Need You," *Sports Illustrated*, 1 October 1984, 89.

Notes

4. Richard N. Goldstein, "Cable, Disc, and All That Jazz: A Labor Relations Saga," *ILR Report* (New York State School of Industrial and Labor Relations, Cornell University) 21, no. 2 (Spring 1984): 13.

5. William Taaffe, "TV/Radio," *Sports Illustrated*, 2 April 1984, 78.

6. "Double Play," *Time*, 14 May 1984, 53.

7. See James W. Quinn and Irwin H. Warren, "Professional Team Sports' New Legal Arena: Television and the Players' Right of Publicity," *Indiana Law Review* 16, no. 2 (Spring 1983): 487–516.

8. Portions of this section are from Paul D. Staudohar, "Team Relocation in Professional Sports," *Labor Law Journal* 36, no. 9 (September 1985): 728–33.

9. Joe Marcin, "College Football Notebook," *Sporting News*, 11 November 1984, 36.

10. Ronald A. DiNicola and Scott Mendeloff, "Controlling Violence in Professional Sports: Rule Reform and the Federal Professional Sports Violence Commission," *Duquesne Law Review* 21, no. 4 (Summer 1983): 843–916.

11. For further discussion of media impacts on sports personalities, see Benjamin G. Rader, *In Its Own Image: How Television Has Transformed Professional Sports* (New York: Free Press, 1984), 175–95.

12. An interesting description of the sources of fan alienation can be found in John Underwood, *Spoiled Sport: A Fan's Notes on the Troubles of Spectator Sports* (Boston: Little, Brown and Company, 1984), 59–78.

Name Index

183

Name Index

Name Index

Subject Index

Subject Index